QUITE ALONE

Journalism from the Middle
East 2008-2019

Matthew Teller

Cover: St George Monastery, Wadi Qelt, Palestine © Matthew Teller

ISBN 979-8-67190-964-7 (paperback)

Independently published
www.matthewteller.com

To my father, and in memory of my mother

*To the people of the region, for their kindness and
hospitality*

To I and I: we will travel again

To Hannah, for everything

To awaken quite alone in a strange town is one of the pleasantest sensations in the world. You are surrounded by adventure. You have no idea of what is in store for you, but you will, if you are wise and know the art of travel, let yourself go on the stream of the unknown and accept whatever comes in the spirit in which the gods may offer it.

FREYA STARK, 'BAGHDAD SKETCHES' (1937)

CONTENTS

PREFACE

These are stories of people, not war or geopolitics. I'm astonishingly lucky to have been travelling to, living in and writing about the Middle East for four decades. It's been, literally, a privilege. I've loved just about every minute of it, and want to share my memories of the beauty, diversity, creativity and inspiration I found there. This selection of some of what I've written over the last twelve years is a way to say thank you, to the place but above all to the people who showed me such extraordinary hospitality over all that time. (I've got plenty more stuff squirrelled away that's even older, too, but on balance, let's not go there.)

"Middle East" doesn't mean much. The term was invented a little over a hundred years ago by British and American military officials, and has served different purposes at different times, sometimes excluding Egypt, or even Syria, at other times stretching to include Afghanistan and even Tibet. There has never been agreement on exactly which countries it covers. And, of course, it epitomises a long outdated, orientalist world view centred on Europe. It implies a "Near East", but that term has fallen out of usage, in Britain at least—and a "Far East", but that is now East Asia. In response some academics and international organisations rename the Middle East "West Asia" or "Southwest Asia", but neither has stuck with most people who live there and, anyway, "Asia" is itself a problematic term, its modern usage also rooted in orientalism. Another circumlocution, MENA ("the Middle East and North Africa"), is slowly being supplanted by WANA ("West Asia and North Africa") or even SWANA ("South-West Asia and..."). But in Arabic as in English, "Middle East" is still preferred. So, for now, for the purposes of this book, "Middle East" will do.

There are published pieces here from every country in the region between Egypt and Oman—bar Yemen, which I'm sorry to say I have never yet visited and which now endures the world's worst humanitarian crisis, brought on by a civil war exacerbated by military interventions from, among others, Saudi Arabia, the UAE, Iran, Britain, France and the US. Yemenis' suffering shames humanity. In the midst of the pandemic, as we face battles against racism, fascism, corporate manipulation and political incompetence, as accountability recedes, as hard-won rights are dismantled and intolerance gains new legitimacy, please don't forget Yemen.

Some of what I wrote here I wouldn't write today, or at least not in the same way. Nevertheless, apart from a bit of light editing for clarity I've left my words alone. These articles were commissioned by different outlets, with different preoccupations and diverse readerships—some are tales of travel, some are profiles of individuals, some are examinations of single issues—but if they have a common thread, I hope it will be discernible as a desire to amplify the voices of the overlooked and the underserved, and thereby tell some new stories about place. I got into travel writing because I could see how damaging the stereotypes were that my generation held about the Middle East. I wanted to help demolish them, and was able to build myself a platform from which to attempt that. Today, some years on, the current generation sees more clearly than we did, I think, and has rightly grown tired of the opinions of white men who travel the world passing judgement on others. I hope that such a sense of entitlement is absent here, even if it's clear there's more I could have done to accelerate that cleansing process of demolition. Luckily, I still have time.

* * *

One last word. Like all journalists doing similar work, much of what I do relies on guides and fixers. Often journalists in their own right, these professional people live and work in the places I am sent to. Their job—for an hour, a day, a week, whatever it takes—is to help me, in some places with translation or navigation, in others with local knowledge or contacts, or the ability to open closed doors. Some of these pieces I wrote alone; others would never have seen the light of day without the help and support of guides and fixers. For their role in shaping and informing opinion around the world they are indispensable, and too often unacknowledged.

Journalism's greatest recent advance has been that these experts are employed less and less as guides and fixers, and more and more as narrators and journalists in their own right. Countries—and people—that looked to others to tell their stories for them, or that struggled to be heard at all, are telling their own stories, their way. Such a redistribution of power is good for everyone.

The next step is for media newsrooms and, especially,

media boardrooms to catch up and start redistributing their own power to match. We all need some new stories from them.

Matthew Teller
Banbury, UK
August 2020
matthewteller.com

EGYPT: "THIS ISN'T A TEMPLE, IT'S A PHILOSOPHY"

Travel / 2013 / Wanderlust

Temple fatigue. It afflicts us all. This pharaoh, that goddess, some dynasty or other. More columns, more carvings. It's embarrassing, to be bored by something you know is wondrous.

And then, one bright day, up pops the antidote.

"Come and see!"

His name is Hesham Mansoor, and he may be the best history guide in Egypt. In Hesham's world, every moment holds a story worth telling.

Amid the gloom of the great temple at Abydos he led a huddle of us onward with a whisper. "This is really a wow scene."

A histrionic sunbeam was doing the Indiana Jones thing, slanting dustily down from far overhead to spotlight an ankle-high patch of wall-carving. The hum of voices was retreating. At a place of sacred pilgrimage three thousand years old we were face to face with the gods.

And in amongst the flow of bulls and hieroglyphs, cartouches and almond eyes, Hesham picked out a single bas-relief. Beside falcon-headed Horus, eerily transcendent, stood two wasp-waisted figures, their hair, faces and fingernails carved with ancient, intimate perfection.

"Renpet, goddess of the year, and Maat, goddess of truth," cooed Hesham. "They are telling us that Horus is always honest. Just look at these beautiful ladies. You have nothing to do but love them."

And we did.

Again, under fierce sun before the immense mortuary temple of Queen Hatshepsut in Luxor. As glistening busloads trudged to their photo-ops, Hesham took us aside.

"You know, this isn't a temple," he said, rising on his toes to gesture at the columned terraces. "It's a philosophy. Death did not scare the Egyptians. You can feel the smile on Hatshepsut's face here. Let me amaze you—listen."

And deftly, passionately, with pacing and arm-waving, Hesham brought the ideas hidden in those hot, old stones to life before our eyes.

We lucked out with Hesham, for sure. But in truth this was never going to be an ordinary temple-hopping tour.

The story starts in 1992. Back then, during a violent insurgency against the Egyptian government, the Gamaa Islamiyya ("Islamic Group") began targeting tourists. Militants attacked buses, trains and boats, killing foreigners and Egyptians alike. The horror culminated in a massacre of 62 people at Hatshepsut's temple in 1997 which outraged public opinion across Egypt and paralysed the country's tourist industry for years afterwards. By that time the Egyptian government had already halted tourism in the whole central section of the country. Nile cruises and organised excursions to sites between Cairo and Luxor were stopped altogether, and independent travellers who chose to venture to Middle Egypt cities such as Minya or Asyut found their movements heavily restricted by the police.

Tourism became concentrated in Cairo, the Red Sea coast and the south. Nile cruises focused solely on the southern stretch of river between Luxor and Aswan. Even after 2003, with the insurgency defeated and the Gamaa Islamiyya renouncing violence, river journeys south from Cairo remained a memory.

It was the 2011 revolution which prompted a rethink. Amid drastic falls in tourism and deepening economic hardship among tourism-reliant communities in Upper Egypt—plus broad consensus that the threat to foreigners has passed—politicians finally approved a relaunch for the once-popular river route. The first public cruise from Cairo to Aswan in two decades set sail on 19th April this year [2013]. I was lucky enough to be on board.

First, let me reassure readers who aren't fans of cruise tourism: neither am I. But oh my goodness! What a soul-stirring marvel of a journey this was. The author Michael Haag takes a cerebral tone in his brilliant guidebook, published by Cadogan, purring, "It is godly to cruise the Nile through Egypt." But for a cruise virgin like myself, being kissed for the very first time by a thousand kilometres of the most famous river in the world made for an earthy old knee-trembler of a fortnight. It was travel of the most stimulating, seductive, deliciously slow kind.

Worlds revealed themselves minute by minute.

Women washed morning pots at the water's edge in village after cruelly underdeveloped village. Hoopoes took flight. Fishermen heaved at plank-like oars. The banks narrowed, so the groves of banana and sugarcane felt a stone's throw away. Then they widened, casting the whistles of children by tall-chimneyed brick kilns faint on the breeze. On one side, long-horned buffalo lounged on sweet rugs of grass, backed by moptop palms. On the other, a Coptic monastery wedged into a fold of desert hills turned its cupola-point cross to face the water.

Despite an air-conditioned cabin, five-star service, an abundance of food and a near-total lack of responsibility, I didn't want to relax. Mid-conversation below decks, I'd catch myself wondering what was floating past unseen. I could only skim-read, with half an eye on the view. Others snoozed shadily, but I'd be at the rail in velvet heat, watching a local ferry load up with farm trucks as be-robed men gossiped by the wheelhouse, or following a migrant glossy ibis as it swooped against the mango trees. I often woke early, standing to catch drifting views alone in the sunrise cool.

Every archaeological excursion—and there were sixteen—was a winner. Thanks chiefly to Hesham's narrative talent, Egypt's endless tide of gods and pharaohs finally made sense to me, our drift southwards matching the chronological sweep from Old Kingdom pyramids at Giza to Middle Kingdom tombs at Beni Hassan, and then New Kingdom temples at Amarna and Luxor.

What made the history click was a meticulously planned itinerary. I'm no great fan of package tours, but it quickly became obvious that to see what we saw in those once-prohibited regions of Middle Egypt would have been nigh-on impossible without the backing of a tour company.

Beni Hassan is a case in point. These stunningly decorated tombs, cut into rocky cliffs high above the eastern bank of the Nile 250 kilometres south of Cairo, were once accessible only by private taxi (with police escort) from Minya, a city nearby that was itself closed to tourists until relatively recently. Our ship, though, had clearance to dock in Minya overnight. By seven in the morning, our convoy of coaches and minibuses was sweeping past the bleary eyes and open mouths of outlying villagers direct to the site.

From a high ledge by the tombs' entrance, the strip of cultivation flanking the Nile—matching the extent of the river's annual flooding, which laid rich, dark soil over otherwise barren desert—shone electric-green against the dusty beige of the wilderness beyond.

Within the tombs, scenes of wrestling—two figures grappling across the walls, as if on celluloid film—were outdone by one of the most famous scenes in Egyptian art. Around 1890 BCE, it seems, a caravan from Canaan—that is, Palestine—visited the pharaoh, bringing gifts. The foreigners are depicted at Beni Hassan with unusual goatee beards, wearing sandals (Egyptians went barefoot) and dressed in striking multicoloured robes. Nobody is suggesting they are Israelites, but Joseph—known, too, for a coat of many colours—was in Egypt around the same time. The parallels with the Old Testament story rang like a bell. It was my turn to gaze openmouthed.

Hesham, once he'd told the tale, shrugged and smiled.

Our convoy whisked us to the beauty of remote Tuna El Gebel, its angular stone mausolea enormously romantic in the afternoon sun against tawny dunes, hair-raising catacombs beneath filled with mummified baboons sacrificed to Thoth, god of knowledge.

In farflung Tell El Amarna we roamed the sun-temple, built 3,400 years ago by the revolutionary pharaoh and queen Akhenaten and Nefertiti. Their newly egalitarian forms of government and worship lasted barely two decades in the teeth of a furious hardline counter-revolution. Pacing the rubble of betrayed dreams, I bit my lip for Tahrir Square.

And then we returned to the river. Excursions fell between mesmerically long stretches of cruising. Hours would pass navigating an inch on the map. Our ship, the MS *Hamees*, was limited to fifteen knots (roughly eight miles per hour), but that wasn't nearly slow enough.

Once, close to Esna, I experimented with real-time writing. First I logged a range of sawtooth cliffs rearing up on the western shore, topped by a squat, domed lookout. They were still passing when I noted a photogenic pair of date palms, one resting on its neighbour's shoulder. I broke off for the putt-putt-putt of a mudbrick pumping station on the opposite shore, drawing water up to cascade into beige irrigation channels. Before that faded, six or seven kids were leaping off a grassy bank, their bodies slick in the afternoon sun. A buffalo bathed, snorting in the shallows. Then came a picnicking family, whooping as our five-storey mobile hotel rudely parped.

Worlds kept revealing themselves, every minute. The whole two weeks was the same.

Life on board had its own rhythm. The ship's seventy-five crew were tending just eighty-three passengers (from a maximum capacity of 142), mostly British, with a small group from Germany and two Swiss. We ate unadventurous food at the same times each day throughout the voyage—soups, salads, veal, beef, chicken, grilled fish, buttery rice, steamed broccoli, half-a-dozen puddings—served by the same waiter at the same table. We took tea and biscuits on the sundeck every afternoon. Sweaty after each excursion, we reboarded to be handed scented face-towels and camomile tea.

Tap water for washing and cleaning was triple-filtered from the Nile, through sand, carbon and ultraviolet, but the cooks prepared all our food with bottled mineral water. Cabins offered picture windows and satellite TV. Haggle-free shops on board sold silk scarves, picture books and jewellery. Laptop dongles provided internet access through local 3G, though I bought an Egyptian sim and cheap data plan for my smartphone instead.

It was gilded, but it was a cage. On the river we'd be hailed every few minutes by calls, whistles and waves from bankside farmers, unused to the sight of cruise ships in the tourist-free districts of Middle Egypt. Some of us waved back. A few even shouted thank yous. To be considered exotic felt therapeutic, but there was no chance to explain. The ship never stopped, the cheers inexorably faded and we were always left alone with ourselves, our paperbacks and our smoked salmon.

On land, our buses left hamlets coughing as we roared, inviolate, from ship to ruin and back. We could watch rural Egypt, but not touch. Contact, even when it came, was mediated. As the souvenir touts crowded around, Hesham would gather armfuls of scarves and scarabs, take them—and us—back to the sanctuary of the bus, and then pass money and unbought merchandise back out through the open door. It was useful, but I missed the banter of a haggle. Eventually, I sloped off to do my own deals.

The ship never had fewer than four armed police on board. Each day police boats took turns to bounce along in our wake, and each night our gangplank was guarded by men with brass buttons and epaulettes.

"We're treading on eggshells," the ship manager told me. "This is the first trip, so nothing can go wrong. Things will ease up a bit."

I was permitted to amble around the squares and souks of Beni Suef and Asyut only if hard-eyed police followed three paces behind.

A couple of times I gave them the slip. In Minya, where a swanky new archaeology museum is due to open, I roamed a city centre as charming as anywhere in Egypt. A 20th-century cotton capital, exporting to Europe and beyond, Minya sings with the textile magnates' colonial Rococo and Art Deco villas, many now artfully crumbling. Stares broke into smiles at my "*as-salaamu alaykum*". Fathers nudged their moon-eyed children. Lads jostled for photos.

Dodging taxis emblazoned with Jesus stickers—Minya's population is roughly half Christian, half Muslim—I stopped for tea off the main square. A dreadlocked hipster was talking to a blonde woman—his sister? girlfriend?—in sign language. A passing cigarette-seller boomed in Arabic, "Foreigners are welcome." The guy over the road smoking a water-pipe pointed and waved. The tea cost me 20p.

When I lived in Cairo in 1993, only journalists visited Asyut, preferably in body-armour. Times have changed. My Rough Guide enthused about Asyut's Qasreya souk: "A web of shadowy lanes smelling of incense and offal," it said. I asked the dockside police how to get there. After their initial surprise ("How does he know about

Qasreya?" I overheard), one agreed to take me. It was sensational. Forests of cotton-polyester draped broken alleys in day-glo. There were saucepans, spice grinders and plenty of raised eyebrows, as coffeeshop loafers registered a tourist in their souk. Shouldering between cobblers and herb-sellers, I—literally—stumbled into a medieval wooden-galleried caravanserai, unrestored and gloomy, perhaps from the miserable days when Asyut hosted the biggest slave market in Africa. By midnight I was sipping tea on a packed café terrace, while music played and laughter danced over the implacable Nile. The cruise had unlocked a whole new Egypt for me.

For Egyptians, times are as hard as they've ever been. Of six thousand tour guides nationwide, five and a half thousand are out of work. Fewer than a quarter of the Nile's three hundred cruise ships are operating. Nine out of ten hotel rooms in Luxor are empty. There are long queues for petrol. People are skipping meals. The country may be going through political transition but that shouldn't be a stick for us to beat it with. Quite the opposite. Planes are flying. Tours are running. Prices are low. Sites are quiet.

And Egypt's spirit, of course, remains undaunted. At Meidum, our excursion to the 4,600-year-old Collapsed Pyramid happened to coincide with National Orphans' Day. Beneath the high old walls girls in yellows, blues and pinks twirled together, clapping and chanting on their day out from school. Boys posed, one or two boldly asking my name. A teacher shook my hand.

"We're happy that you come to visit us in such circumstances," he said. "You are fighters, really."

But it didn't feel like a fight at all. In truth, it felt silky smooth.

Asyut, Minya and the other cities of Middle Egypt, for so long denied the opportunity for tourism growth, now, finally, have a chance. This cruise links them with Cairo and Luxor in an entirely new way, on a single, hassle-free itinerary. They benefit from the cruise companies, who take on supplies mid-voyage. They should also benefit from tourist footfall.

Beside the din of a street-wedding in Qena, a greybeard clasped my elbow in solemn greeting. In the echoing souks of Luxor and Aswan, forlorn shopkeepers brought me tea. Everyone was angry that protests limited to a small zone around Tahrir Square, hundreds of kilometres away, should still be blighting the whole country's prospects.

"I want to cry," one told me. "Egypt is dying."

I promised him I'd get the word out.

EGYPT: POSTCARD FROM QENA

Politics & society / 2013 / i

Qena lurks on the edge of things. This southern Egyptian city stands close enough to the tourist hotels of Luxor—sixty-odd kilometres—that nobody stays, but far enough away that nobody visits either.

Tour buses sweeping in from the Red Sea coast head straight for King Tut's tomb, bypassing Qena. Itineraries to the temple of the love-goddess Hathoor, at Dendara nearby, include direct transport from Luxor by bus or boat—though these days there's precious little demand.

What's so awful about Qena that passers-by always detour?

I walked on neat, shaded streets, causing cheerful pavement jams by stopping to chat with doorway loafers.

Ex-governor Adel Labib is credited with giving Qena some spit and polish after the devastating Islamist insurgency of the 1990s, building civic participation in schemes from fixing rubbish collections to launching a women's football team.

Labib, with a background in state security, was rewarded by former president Hosni Mubarak with a transfer to Alexandria. He was governor there in 2010 when activist Khaled Said was beaten to death by police—one of the sparks for the Egyptian revolution. Days after Mubarak resigned the presidency in February 2011, Labib resigned his governorship.

He wasn't gone long. Six months later, Egypt's ruling military council sent him back to Qena—only for him to be kicked out by ex-president Morsi last month, a fortnight before Morsi himself was ejected from office [on July 3rd 2013]. The new governor, Salah Abdel-Meguid, lasted 22 days; he resigned on Monday morning [July 8th 2013].

Regardless, Qena's big families keep the streets calm. On a warm night in the main square, a group of teenagers around a booming sound system is drawing a crowd with backflips and '80s-style bodypopping. Tambourines and trumpets fanfaring a street wedding add to the cacophony of car horns.

Insulated against tourist no-shows and ruled by familiar faces, Qena is like the revolution never happened.

LEBANON: FINDING THE ESSENCE

Culture / 2010 / AramcoWorld

In west Beirut, Hamra Street's fashion boutiques and upmarket coffee shops form a strip of commerce, pointing the way toward the landmark Murr Tower on the edge of the downtown area. A block or two north, past clusters of car workshops and convenience stores, lies the residential neighborhood of Jounblat. Here, on quiet, narrow America Street, you may find an anonymous dead-end that snakes away between apartment blocks.

Down an alley off an alley, reached by a side-street off a side-street, lives Mona Saudi, artist, poet, and sculptor.

"I'm in the city," she says, gesturing around her leafy, hidden garden, lemons hanging over cacti, "but as you can see—I'm also not!"

Still living in the modest 19th-century house she

rented first in 1974, then later bought, Saudi surrounds herself with her work: abstract sculptures fill a little terrace space among the trees, deceptively light pieces in fluently carved limestone and marble, some graspable in two hands, others soaring above head height, offsetting the natural disorder. They look graceful enough to fly, but most would no doubt require a crane to shift. She places a hand on one of her sculptures as she explains how important it is for her to have space for contemplation, adding, "I need seclusion. I need birdsong."

In a charming, unexpected haven amid the noisiest of cities, this ground-breaking artist has found both.

* * *

Mona Saudi was born in Amman on October 1st, 1945, at a time when the Jordanian capital was barely more than a village. She grew up in a family of eight siblings, and recalls playing as a child among the tumbled columns and blocks of the Nymphaeum, a semi-ruined Roman fountain near their home in the city centre— doubtless a deeply impressive structure.

It was apparent early on that she was determined to make her own way. "From the age of 6 or 7 I wanted to be a creative person, free," Saudi says. "My first feelings were towards being earthy."

She was a voracious reader, frequently visiting Amman's British Council library and absorbing T.S. Eliot's poem of moral decay *The Waste Land* at the age of 14, "even before I started reading Arab poetry," she says. She names Colin Wilson's 1956 study of alienation *The Outsider* as a key early influence.

"It was very important to have read that," she says.

"Wilson examined so many artists and thinkers who broke with tradition: Nietzsche, Rilke, Joyce, Rimbaud. For me, this was the discovery of a global way of thinking."

The poetry magazine *Shi'r*, published in Beirut, helped Saudi make the link to Arab literary traditions. As well as publishing Western writers in translation, *Shi'r* showcased contemporary Arab poets such as Yousef al-Khal and Adonis. Saudi acknowledges that it inspired her to begin writing her own poetry.

Such precociousness inevitably led to tensions at home: the artist's younger sister Fathieh, now a published poet, laughs as she remembers family life being "war every day!" When Saudi—by then dressed entirely in black, under influence from existentialist philosophy —was forbidden by her father to apply for university, she took the momentous decision to drop out of high school and escape Amman for the freer, more progressively minded city of Beirut. As she wrote later in her monograph *Forty Years in Sculpture*: "That day my life began."

The Lebanese capital, which Saudi recalls as "vivid... a large space of contemplation and continual movement", made a lifelong impression. She used her time in Beirut to make contact with the city's artistic underground and mount her first exhibit of paintings, at the Café de la Presse in Hamra.

The proceeds allowed Saudi to put even more distance between herself and her upbringing: she bought a ticket to Paris. "I went by sea," she smiles. "I had been dreaming of going to Paris since I was a child, and to realise my dream it seemed appropriate to travel through water."

Even today, sipping tea in her garden, remembering that epic voyage makes her laugh with pleasure. Following stops at several Mediterranean ports and an overnight train ride from Marseilles, Saudi arrived in Paris on a cold February morning in 1964. She went straight to the only address she knew, that of Lebanese artist Halim Jurdak, whom Saudi had met the year before in Beirut.

"It was early morning," Saudi recalls. "He came down the stairs, so astonished to see this girl from Jordan on his doorstep. He took me to a small hotel in the Saint Germain quarter—I remember it was unheated and cost four francs a night [about one US dollar]."

Saudi was accepted into Paris's famous School of Fine Arts, where she began to experiment with sculpture. Her first work in stone, *Mother/Earth*, is dated 1965. A single block of limestone comprising two bulging volumes flanking a spherical form, it announces many of the themes and preoccupations that would mark Saudi's career, chief among them fertility. Saudi's focus on the embrace-like interaction of spheres within semi-circles, and her ability to draw organic, curvaceous warmth out of cold stone, express an inner energy which recurs throughout her oeuvre. This is made explicit by the work's title, a juxtaposition of terms to which Saudi returned repeatedly in a series of *Mother/Earth* sculptures over subsequent decades.

One of the strongest influences on her style—acknowledged both by the artist herself and by observers—has been the Romanian sculptor Constantin Brancusi (1876-1957), specifically Brancusi's stated desire to sculpt "not the appearance, but the idea, the essence of things". Saudi's 1970 piece *Lovers* makes the debt clear, its sinuous, elongated forms stretching upwards in a lithe embrace. As Paul Richard of the Washington Post commented: "[Saudi's] stone pieces, like [Brancusi's], simultaneously suggest the ageless and the modern." "Mona Saudi begins with the modernism of Brancusi and Hans Arp," Mazen Asfour, assistant dean in the Faculty of Fine Arts at Jordan University in Amman, tells me. "Lyric abstraction with touches of Cubism—and she mixes it with humanism. She is looking for a dialogue [by using] dimensional tricks: the illusion of space within her sculpture. She draws the viewer in. She wants you to build her form with her."

This "illusion of space", influenced by the English sculptors Barbara Hepworth (1903-1975) and Henry Moore (1898-1986), is a key marker of Saudi's style. In many of her works, pregnant bulges seem to swell from the stone, hinting at egg-like fertility as well as at interior voids. Saudi has her own way of describing this: "I start with a block," she says, "and I have to open distances within it. I put time inside the stone by dividing it. This is what makes the mystery of sculpture."

Though Saudi stayed in Beirut after the outbreak of civil war, she was eventually persuaded in 1983 to leave for the safety—and family ties—of Amman. By then she was exploring working in different stones, always local to the region: black diorite from Syria, Yemeni alabaster, honey-coloured Lebanese marble and a extraordinary green veined marble from the deserts south of Amman which Saudi has dubbed 'Jordanian jade'.

A series of landscape works in this 'jade', including *Sunrise* (1980) and *Dawn* (1981), as well as later pieces such as *Nocturne* (2002), extends the solid/void juxtaposition: Saudi renders the sky in polished stone, with the earth and sun shaped as empty air. The Lebanese artist and critic Samir Sayegh describes Saudi "using the concept of geometry to express spirituality."

The artist explored the same idea again for her most famous work, *The Geometry of the Soul* (1987), a marble sculpture some ten feet in height donated by Jordan to the Arab World Institute in Paris, where it remains on public display. Drawing together numerous influences—including elements from the ancient art of the Nabataeans, builders of Petra, wave-like undulations reminiscent of the sea or the desert, curved forms which hint at the crescent moon and the suggestion of a musical stave or the strings of an oud—*The Geometry of the Soul* uses an interplay of horizontals and verticals to express both calmness and profundity. Critic Joseph Tarrab spoke of its being "rooted in the persistence of a state both primitive and definitive, the immutability of a basic, absolute permanence".

Another landmark work of the 1980s was *Variations on Arabic 'N'* (1981), a marble piece later installed in the garden of the French Embassy in Amman. The Arabic letter *noon* is formed by a semicircle enclosing a point, embodying Saudi's preoccupation with the embrace-like dialogue between line and sphere, and its sound also often denotes the feminine form of personal pronouns in Arabic (*hunna* is "they" in the feminine). Here, three of these volumes—termed *noon an-niswa*, the women's *noon*—climb to form a figure that is at once totem-like and human, symbolic and figurative.

Yet despite successes abroad throughout the 1980s and 1990s, including exhibits in Washington, London and Paris, Saudi felt cloistered and restricted in Amman. Several projects, including a plan to establish a sculpture centre, foundered. In 1996, three years after receiving Jordan's National Honorary Award for the Arts from King Hussein, she returned to Lebanon.

The last decade has seen Saudi teaching several semesters at the American University in Beirut and participating in high-profile exhibitions, including the 2006 inaugural sale of modern and contemporary art at Christie's in Dubai. She has published editions of her own poetry and has produced series of drawings in ink which combine poems by Adonis, Mahmoud Darwish and the French writer Saint-John Perse with representations of her sculptural forms on paper.

Recent sculptural works show development toward a new sense of fluidity: Her series *Woman/River* as well as individual pieces such as *Woman/Bird* (1998) and *Woman/Water* (2004), with their deployment of wavy silhouettes against solid-edged volumes, deepen impressions of the intangible bonds between the human and the natural world. Saudi's Brancusi-inspired desire to sculpt "the essence of things" is becoming ever more apparent.

✳ ✳ ✳

One of the very few Arab women artists to pursue sculpture, Mona Saudi is acknowledged as a pioneer of Jordanian art, alongside figures such as Nabil Shehadeh, Salah Abu Shindi and the country's most prominent and successful painter Mohanna Durra. She has also stuck tight over five decades to her independence and what Joseph Tarrab has called her "strongly singular" vision, largely heedless of the ebb and flow of artistic fashions.

Durra—under whom Saudi trained in the early 1960s —recognizes the value of such perseverance. "Even back then," he says, "I could tell she had a mind of her own. But that rebellious spirit is also a renovating spirit. I find her work uplifting. She broke taboos and went far beyond

Jordan. Her achievement is great."

Dr Khalid Khreis, director-general of Jordan's National Gallery, concurs, calling Saudi "one of the most important Arab artists", emphasizing her universality and her modernist authenticity.

Yet her work, lacking narrative symbolism and any sign of traditional Arab styles, is not easy to pigeonhole —and the question of her influence on contemporary sculpture remains open: as Barbara Rowell, owner of the Jacaranda gallery in Amman, notes, few contemporary Arab artists are drawing influence or inspiration from Saudi. Sculpture in stone has become deeply unfashionable.

"Defending your obsession like this is not easy. Mona Saudi is one of a generation of artists who fought for art that is international but inspired by local sources," says Saleh Barakat, owner of Beirut's prominent Agial gallery and an expert on contemporary Arab art. "The legacy of Arab culture is within her. She is someone who did not make a career in Europe—it was not open to her—but she has gone around the world, seen, absorbed, digested and produced. She is a lady of the earth."

Despite her youthful defiance—Saudi took part in the 1968 student uprising in Paris and was involved with Palestinian revolutionaries in Lebanon—this angry young artist was eventually reconciled with her parents. She describes her father Abdulmajid as mystical. "He was a religious man, in a different world," she says. "I respected his beliefs, but didn't feel the need to ask his permission."

By contrast she found great inspiration from her mother Yusra, a quiet woman who loved gardening and who, Mona's sister Fathieh notes, often chose to be seen in public deliberately bare-headed, in contravention of social norms. "I feel her love even now," says Saudi. "I feel her protection."

Although married for a time to journalist Hassan Batal, who still writes a daily column for the Palestinian newspaper *Al-Ayyam*—their daughter, Dia Batal, is a professional designer—Saudi has long lived alone. She rarely cooks, preferring to order meals for delivery from the famous Barbar restaurant near her home in Beirut. She works in her little garden, accompanied by CDs of the Canadian pianist Glenn Gould playing Bach ("Very abstract," she smiles. "Bach reflects something geometrical in nature, and listening to Gould is like polishing a sculpture. Each line in its place.") while also spending long hours at a studio she rents in the suburb of Ouzai, a neighbourhood of car repair workshops, carpentry businesses and small factories.

"I'm a dreamer," says the soon-to-be 65-year-old. "I began my life by dreaming, and I still dream today of more sculptures, more exhibits, more discoveries. I don't think of time as a burden: when I was 17 I felt much older than I do now. I still have a lot of things to do."

SYRIA: SUGAR AND SPICE

Travel / 2008 / Guardian/Observer

They were country boys up for a day in the big city—three farmhands, in shabby robes, each with his head untidily wrapped in a red-and-white headcloth. I watched them moving in a tight trio through the Aleppo souk, taking in all the sights and sounds, their faces painted with the wide-eyed gape of newcomers.

As they came to an intersection, with people flowing around them, they stopped, lost. It was a real-life comedy moment.

"Where are we?" I heard one mutter.

"Dunno," shrugged his mate.

The third pointed down a lane. "Let's go this way!"

And they vanished into the crowds.

Everyone's a tourist these days.

If you've never visited Syria, whatever you've heard about the place is quite likely to be wrong. To start with, there's a more tangible air of menace in Guildford, not to mention a greater chance of being caught up in trouble. I did not, regrettably, get to ride on the spanking new high-speed trains, built in South Korea, which have just entered service on the Damascus-Aleppo run, but their presence—even in what remains a corrupt, repressive dictatorship—demonstrates a degree of business confidence and social mobility. The internet is everywhere, fast and reliable, regrettably just like the secret police.

A friend had arranged a room for me at the gallery-cum-workshop of sculptor Mustafa Ali, in the heart of Damascus's crumbling Jewish Quarter. Almost all Syria's Jews departed in the early 1990s, after a long campaign for exit visas. The district lay semi-abandoned until Mustafa bought and renovated one of the old houses in 2004. Now there are more than twenty-five artists in the area and the mood is one of self-reliant dynamism, building a cultural community beyond the reach of ossified state institutions.

As we were chatting over tea in the sculpture-strewn courtyard one afternoon, an old lady popped in to boil a kettle. "Rosa, my neighbour," said Mustafa. "One of the last Jews in Damascus. I open my doors and anyone can visit me."

Another expression of that cosmopolitan outlook is the souk, which I was in Syria to explore alongside Anissa Helou, chef, broadcaster and writer on the cuisines of the Mediterranean.

A Londoner for twenty years, Anissa grew up in Beirut but remembers childhood summers spent in the Syrian highlands. Now she is returning to launch small-group culinary tours, taking ingredients, cooking styles and methods of production as a starting point from which to explore.

Admiring Damascus's historical monuments, or taking time to appreciate the splendid architecture, was firmly off the agenda. Instead, we scoured the souk. I watched as Anissa strode through the crowded lanes, casting to left and right, stopping to see how an old man fries omelettes, pausing to ask a passer-by how she prepares her vegetables, picking out oranges piled on a barrow.

I followed her into the back lanes where we discovered a half-hidden factory making sugared almonds, a single bare room lined with great copper drums for turning the toasted nuts in syrup. The aptly named manager, Qusay Sukkari (*sukkar* is the Arabic word for sugar—delightfully enough, this was Mr Sweet the Confectioner), welcomed us in and explained the process, but apologised for having none of the product to sample. No matter, we said, and instead nipped round the corner to buy *qatayyif*, sweet pastries filled with clotted cream, deep-fried to a crunch and drenched in treacle. Old-fashioned calories matter here. You're never far from a snack in Damascus.

And there's little reverence for the city's immense history. At Beit Shami, a restaurant occupying a magnificent traditional courtyard residence dating from the 13th century, a spattering marble fountain was competing for attention with giant plasma screens fixed on each wall blaring a music video channel. The dapper Jordanian *maitre d'*, Mazen, did his best to keep up appearances, gliding over as I sipped my post-prandial infusion of jasmine blossom to offer an extra dessert of five Syrian marmalades on hand-baked melba toast. "No charge," he flapped his hands deferentially while Lebanese singers warbled on the screen above him.

Damascus was a relevation. I'd visited before, but never with the sole purpose of shopping. I followed as Anissa plunged into the Souk al-Bzouriya ('Seeds Market'), buying up *zaatar*, a blend of thyme, marjoram and sesame, sniffing perfumes and sampling boiled sweets. And it was my first time at the fascinating Souk al-Tanabel ('Lazybones Market'), where stallholders sell bagged, pre-prepared vegetables to busy mums—sliced carrots, cored squash, chopped herbs: convenience shopping, Syrian-style.

We stopped at streetside stalls to taste mulberry juice, fresh sugar-cane juice and a bitter, black liquid squeezed from liquorice root, and then headed over to Ghraoui, Syria's leading confectioner, for simply scrumptious Damascene candied apricots.

And we ate in a succession of fabulous restaurants —Al-Khawali, for one. Occupying an eye-popping 14th-century palace in the heart of the Damascus souk, this mainstay of Syrian power-dining stands concealed from the street's bustle by beautifully carved wooden doors. Inside, floors of patterned marble lead to an airy internal courtyard, with tables laid around a central fountain beside jasmine and citrus trees. Anissa ordered a clutch of *mezze*—small, sampler-style dishes that crowded the table with flavours, textures and aromas, ranging from familiar *yalangi* (stuffed vine leaves) to exquisite *shanklish*, a tangy sheep's cheese dusted with pepper and thyme. We dipped and nibbled our way through eight or ten *mezze* dishes, plus mains of tender grilled lamb. The food—formal, sophisticated, charming—suited the ambience perfectly.

Old Town, a rather unimaginatively named restaurant in Damascus's Christian Quarter, was another highlight, serving pungent, fiery *muhammara*—a spicy dip of chopped walnuts and red pepper—and succulent kebabs of chicken. The culinary theme continued in Aleppo, four hours north by road. This trading city—the furthest north in the Arab world, tight against the Turkish frontier—is as old as Damascus, perhaps older. Its Arabic name, *Halab*, derives from *haleeb*, the word for milk: Abraham is supposed to have stopped here to milk his cow. But, again, we weren't here for history.

Instead, the vastly knowledgeable Hassan Khouja, a researcher from the *Académie Syrienne de la Gastronomie* (such a body does exist), led us through the labyrinthine souk to one of the old khans, or merchants' courtyards. We picked a path across the old flagstones to the richly aromatic Akesh sesame workshop, which churns out savoury *tahini* paste and crumbly, super-sweet *halawa*. More tea and high-calorie snacks ensued.

At Bazar ash-Sharq, a restaurant hidden in vaulted cellars just outside the old city walls ("the best kitchen in Aleppo," said gastronome Hassan), we dined on superb *kibbeh nayeh*, raw lamb's meat chopped with spices and burghul, one of the most difficult of mezze dishes to get right. It was superb: soft, moist and earthily flavourful.

As we sampled Aleppan meatballs with quince, Hassan explained how Syria's cuisines vary. Aleppo's location on the east–west Silk Route historically drew in both Persian and Turkish influence, particularly with the mixing of savoury and sweet in the city's trademark spicy kebabs with sour cherries. Damascus, on the other hand, far to the south and cut off from eastern influence by the desert, always looked more to Lebanese mountain cuisine for subtler combinations of vegetables, beans and herbs in mezze dishes and salads.

The difference was still tangible: the *zaatar* we bought in Aleppo was sharper and more peppery than Damascus's, and where our Damascene sweet treats were candied apricots and local ice cream—egg-free and beaten by hand—in Aleppo we were offered elegantly crafted confections of spun sugar with Iranian pistachio nuts.

As well as world-class restaurants, Syria is also starting to take a leaf out of Morocco's boutique-hotel book. The lanes of Damascus's Bab Touma district shelter a number of upmarket conversions of seventeenth- and eighteenth-century courtyard town houses. At Beit al-Mamlouka—the first and still one of the most stylish— all eight bedrooms were all occupied when we visited, but the engaging owner, May Mamarbashi, nonetheless served us tea in the orange-scented courtyard and showed us around, pointing out original features and inviting us to return.

While I plumped for a simple room above sculptor Mustafa Ali's workshop, Anissa stayed first at Dar al-Yasmin, another heritage conversion featuring marble fountains and beautiful pointed arches, then moved to the Talisman, a small hotel converted from a wealthy merchant's residence on a dusty lane in the old Jewish Quarter. The Talisman's French owners have deliberately overlaid the traditional Syrian architecture with a ragbag of design elements: Indian trinkets hang beside Cairene lamps and a Moroccan red wash covers the walls —more gaudy than chic.

More endearing was the Mansouriya Palace, down a narrow alleyway near the medieval Bab Qinisreen gateway in Aleppo's old quarter. Within another serene mansion of white marble, its courtyard shaded by Seville orange trees, we investigated all nine suites, each wildly over-themed to the point of kitsch. The Hittite Suite came complete with stone lions flanking the bed, its bath and sink carved from single blocks of marble, while the Ottoman Suite was dominated by a four-poster bed bedecked in swags of heavy silk.

But the real discovery remained the food. Bypassing Syria's ruins for a ritzy week of near-continuous eating and snacking in the company of an expert turned out to be a great way to get a handle on this often hard-to-fathom country. Food is a field where Syria excels. It seems a shame not to take advantage.

IRAQ: CITADEL OF CULTURE

Kurdish heritage / 2019 / AramcoWorld

In the bazaar, Nuna is worried.

Nuna's shop is small. Just a few metres square, with an open front to the street. Shelves of wood and metal line the rough stone walls, some slumped at an angle, all piled with neatly wound bolts of cloth. Spooled thread rests near at hand as Nuna Issa Nuna, a trim, twinkle-eyed figure in ironed shirt and tweed jacket, sits in his red plastic chair against one wall. A white undershirt shows at his throat. Trimmed white hair shows at his temples, beneath a vividly zigzag-patterned skullcap. A sewing machine before him is threaded and ready to work.

As voices drifted around us from the *Chaikhana Piramerd*, the Tea-House of the Old Men, just across the narrow street, Nuna shifted a pair of oversized tailor's scissors to one side and dropped his hands into his lap.

"There was a time when all the villages around here, hundreds of them, only had this bazaar," he told me, be-

fore embarking on a long story that went from the time
he was a soldier in the Iraqi army in 1949, fighting for
Palestine, to the awful day in 1961 when he had to flee
the bazaar wearing only the clothes on his back because a
mob was on the rampage, setting fires. "I lost all my sewing machines," he said, with a rueful smile.

Nuna returned after seven years' enforced absence,
and has been back in the bazaar since then—but, he said
without rancour, "the taste of life has gone." The bazaar is not what it was. A new strip of shops, over near
the town entrance, is siphoning business away. Lots of
people stay down in the valley now, and don't even
bother to come up to the town at all. What's next? Nuna
isn't sure.

Amedi is changing.

* * *

To Iraqis, Amedi (which is the Kurdish name, stressed
on the first syllable; its Arabic equivalent is al-Amadiya)
is as familiar as Mount Rushmore or Niagara Falls might
be to Americans. Located in the Kurdistan region in
the far north of Iraq, barely fifteen kilometres from
the border with Turkey, the town draws visitors all
summer long—partly for its history, but mainly for its
spectacular natural beauty. Amedi is set 1,400 metres
above sea level, in a landscape of high mountains and
rushing waterfalls. When the rest of Iraq swelters, Amedi
remains cool. People come from Baghdad, Basra and further afield, all across the Gulf, to relax, draw breath and
picnic beside flowing water.

If you approach, as most visitors do, on the narrow
road that clings to the contours of the foothills, pass-

ing through sunlit villages of farms and family commerce, past forests and fruit orchards and the now-empty mountain palace of Iraq's boy king Faisal II (1935–58), you're unlikely to forget your first glimpse of Amedi. Like a ship, this ancient town of only four thousand people rides high above the valley atop its own flat-topped crag—a sheer-sided mesa marooned alone, four hundred metres above a green floor, its elliptical surface tilted towards the road as if to show off its best aspect to newcomers. At its back to the north, Amedi has the barrier of the Mateen range, cresting 3,200 metres on the Turkish border. In front to the south, across the rumpled, ten-kilometre-wide Sopna Mateen valley, watered by runoff streams, looms the wall of the Gara range, almost as high.

Today it's Amedi's setting, and particularly the cluster of mountain resorts nearby—most notably Sulav, a thread of gaudy restaurants and snack outlets which coils between waterfalls at the foot of Amedi's mesa—that draws admiring visitors.

But before the age of tourism, it was Amedi itself, and the appeal of its stupendous, easily defendable location, that drew attention. The first mention in the historical record comes when an Assyrian army captured the rock in the 9th century BCE. Such an attack implies that the site had already been fortified, but by whom? The Assyrians recorded the name of the place as Amadi or Amedi, which to many historians suggests a link with the Medes, a tribal people from northwestern Iran, even though hard evidence that the Medes were in fact Amedi's original population is, so far, lacking.

The Medes eventually took—or retook—Amedi, elevating it to become the second city of their empire. The

Parthians were next, venturing into these mountains two thousand years ago from their power-base in Iran. A larger city than Amedi might have retained evidence of the long periods of Median and Parthian rule, but in this tiny place, restricted to the area of only one square kilometre on the surface of its mesa, space has always been at a premium, and there has been little quarter given to holding onto remnants of the past for their own sake. That has implications for our own time. Building for today has always won out over preservation of yesterday, and still does. If physical evidence of Amedi's long history is not to be lost, intervention is becoming imperative.

Amedi is no museum-piece: it is alive with cafés, fashion boutiques and offices, schoolchildren, doctors and mechanics. But signs of the past are everywhere, if you know where to look. At the southwestern edge of Amedi's mountain, carved into the cliffs that gaze out over the green of the Sopna valley, buttressing the modern houses of the city above, you can still see images of Parthian (or perhaps slightly later—but still pre-Islamic —Sasanian) soldiers, sculpted into niches in the rock. They are double life-size, armed and striding in victory, but also unprotected, exposed to the elements and so heavily eroded.

Townspeople and authorities largely ignore them, and they are also virtually unstudied by historians.

To see them, you must walk out of Amedi through the Mosul Gate, a fortified portal of arched stonework at the top of a steep, twisting, stepped and rocky footpath up from the valley. This is the only one of Amedi's ancient gates still surviving, on the southwestern flank of the mesa facing towards the largest city in the area, Mosul, ninety kilometres away. Carved overhead with wolf-headed serpents, images of the sun and booted warriors, the gateway—its walls an extension of the sheer mountain cliffs—forced invaders to make two steeply ascending ninety-degree turns to enter the city. Impregnability was virtually guaranteed. Though part-destroyed in the 1970s and poorly rebuilt, with blocks inserted higgledy-piggledy and carvings mismatched, the Mosul Gate remains a powerful symbol of the cultural heritage carried by Amedi.

That cultural heritage is growing in importance. The devastating social and cultural upheavals suffered by Iraq during this century and the last have helped spur widespread recognition of the value Iraqis of all backgrounds have long placed on their own history. For Kurds, oppressed harshly under successive Iraqi regimes, cultural heritage has particular poignancy. After widespread campaigning, in 2014 UNESCO inscribed the fortified and restored citadel which rises above the centre of Iraqi Kurdistan's capital, Erbil, on its World Heritage Site list. That success has helped fuel a concerted global effort to raise the profile of cultural heritage preservation across Iraq, particularly in Iraqi Kurdistan.

One example is the British government-funded Nahrein Network, an academic support body set up in 2017 to foster cooperation between Iraqi and British researchers. It is jointly run by teams at the University of Kurdistan Hewlêr (Erbil), University College London and Britain's Ashmolean Museum. Elsewhere, Washington, DC's Smithsonian Institution has been working since 2015 with the Erbil-based Iraqi Institute for the Conservation of Antiquities and Heritage to help build capacity among local heritage experts through workshops and professional courses. The institute's director, Dr Abdullah Khorsheed Qader, was instrumental in the Erbil Citadel restoration and remains closely involved with heritage issues across the country.

"Cultural heritage preservation is all about awareness and education," he told me in the institute's headquarters in downtown Erbil, the day before he was due to fly to Japan to speak at a conference on global concerns for cultural heritage. "I know that my people need to be aware of what our heritage is. That depends on economic buoyancy, which depends on political stability."

According to Dr Qader, Amedi is of "incalculable" value. "We had more than two hundred citadels in Kurdistan. Most were destroyed. But Amedi kept its history in situ."

That history comes to us today mainly from Amedi's 'golden age', when for almost five hundred years this small mountain-top city was the capital of the Bahdinan Emirate, one of a string of semi-independent principalities that threaded the mountains between Turkey and Iran. Founded in 1376 and ruled by a succession of Kurdish nobles who claimed descent from the Abbasid caliphs of Baghdad, the emirate persisted right through to 1843.

"Amedi was the centre, ruling the whole area. The political and administrative position of the city was very high. This is an important part of our history, both Kurdish and Iraqi," says Dr Shireen Younus Ismael, a professor in spatial and urban planning at the University of Duhok (Amedi falls within Duhok's governorate, one of the three provinces of Iraq forming the Kurdistan region).

"In many cities, urban expansion meant that the citadel became part of a bigger city, as in Erbil. But Amedi has kept its original characteristics. It has been used as a fortified citadel for the inhabitants right down to today. This makes it unique. It should be preserved," she adds. Dr Ismael's involvement with Amedi extends back more than a decade. From 2006 to 2009 she presented Amedi as a case study in an international programme run by Dortmund University in Germany. Her often solo lobbying of the authorities at regional and national level, and her research into Amedi's cultural significance, led in 2011 to UNESCO's acceptance of Amedi on Iraq's Tentative List of World Heritage Sites, a preliminary step towards full listing.

What should now follow is a master plan for the city as a whole, pinpointing sites for preservation, areas for development and provision for social and economic growth. All the money and resources have up to now been poured into Erbil but, as Dr Ismael acknowledges, that is changing.

"There is new movement," she says.

Since 2013 the World Monuments Fund (WMF), a New York-based nonprofit that works to preserve cultural heritage sites around the world, had been running training courses at Dr Qader's conservation institute in Erbil. Alessandra Peruzzetto, WMF's Middle East programme specialist, takes up the story.

"While we were there we wanted to include local projects. Someone introduced me to [Dr] Shireen [Younus Ismael]. She gave a lecture in Duhok, then we went to Amedi and she took us around. Everything started from there."

Through Peruzzetto, WMF's London office adopted the idea of a plan to draw funding for heritage conservation in Amedi, bringing in Dr Ismael as coordinator and consultant. "Shireen's vision for Amedi became WMF's

vision," says Peruzzetto. In Iraq and also Syria, the conservation spotlight invariably falls on the larger cities,
with less attention given to "peripheral towns and rural
places." In Dr Ismael, WMF saw an opportunity to correct
that imbalance. In 2016 WMF nominated Amedi to its priori-
tized global Watch List.

Two years later the British
government's Cultural Protection Fund awarded WMF
£100,000 ($129,000) to develop the process of docu-
menting Amedi's heritage that had been begun by Dr
Ismael. Further educational grants have followed from
the European Union. One of the core tasks now is to
strengthen local conservation capacity, currently frag-
mented among government and non-government agen-
cies at levels from municipal to national. To that end, Dr
Ismael has helped lead workshops in Amedi in 2018 and
2019 attended by local students and government staff.

"We, as the Kurdistan region, have been excluded from
these activities for a long time," Dr Ismael says, whose
2014 PhD was the first doctoral degree in conservation
ever accredited in Kurdistan. "We have no sites registered as a historic quarter or historic city. The lists deal
with heritage as individual sites. But as professional conservationists we look at each site in context, developing
different strategies to manage the site in its surroundings."

A key challenge is to marry Amedi's conservation
needs with the needs of its population.

"The people need space, comfortable houses, infrastructure—but they also need work. They can use the
potential the city has to create job opportunities," Dr Ismael says.

* * *

On a chilly morning in autumn, the approach to Amedi winds from the rain-damp restaurants and souvenir displays of Sulav across a saddle to the city's eastern cliff. Here, the stepped footpath of old has been swept away by almost a century of successively ambitious access schemes, culminating in an immaculately engineered and illuminated highway ramp, unveiled in 2016. Cars and pedestrians now enter Amedi at a roundabout junction, and follow the city's only road, a twentieth-century innovation that traces a 1.8-kilometre oval around the mesa's circumference—broad and well-kept.

The sense of civic responsibility is palpable. "Amedi is a city, but what does that mean? To be a city is in your mind. You need education, trade—and you must have culture," says Sayyid Ibrahim, a store owner.

But improving access has resulted in the loss of the Zibar Gate, the Mosul Gate's cross-town twin (Zibar is a village east of Amedi): photographs from 1933 show an arched entrance-way of stone being demolished by a gang of workers before the first road was laid. You can stand today where the Zibar Gate once stood, on an exposed shoulder of the mountain, the remnants of the old sloping road at your feet. Behind you, what was once the main artery into the city is now an alleyway between houses, though the lost geography is still discernible: The road from the Zibar Gate led directly to the mosque —whose stone minaret is in plain sight a few metres ahead—and from there continued as the bazaar street, which cuts a diagonal path across town directly to the Mosul Gate.

The minaret itself is one of Amedi's most prominent landmarks, 31 metres high and built around 450 years ago during the Bahdinan Emirate, while beside the Zibar Gate, their stonework bonded together, once stood the political and administrative center of the city. Known as Emirate House, this two-storey gubernatorial palace fell into ruin as Amedi's power waned in the nineteenth century. In the 1950s a school was built over the ruins, and more remnants were swept away in the 1970s—both political acts of erasure by the Baghdad government. All that survives, wedged between modern walls, is an arch of stone that served as the palace gate, carved overhead with an eagle and two snakes (or, some say, two dragons).

"You see the same creatures on gates in Baghdad, in Sinjar [west of Mosul], in Aleppo [in Syria]," says Dr Qader. "The Kurds were connected. Amedi wasn't remote, it was all the same culture."

But buildings are only part of Amedi's story. At least as important is the city's intangible heritage and, specifically, its reputation for coexistence. Here, as in other cities across Kurdistan, people of different religions lived, worked, played and prayed side by side.

Today, Muslims are in a majority, but around a third of the district's population is Christian: Amedi's thirty or so Christian families still live and worship in what's known as the Christian quarter on the west side of town. For Halbin Ismael, librarian at the Amedi campus of Duhok University, this is a source of pride.

"You can't tell whether a family is Christian or Muslim. Last month there was a Christian funeral, and three-quarters of the mourners were Muslim," she told me.

Nearby, and behind the mosque's towering minaret, extends a cluster of alleyways that long formed Amedi's

Jewish quarter. Jews have lived in Kurdistan perhaps since the time of Nebuchadnezzar, 2,600 years ago. For centuries Amedi was a leading centre of Jewish population. In the twelfth and thirteenth centuries the community supported two synagogues. Half-hidden today amongst the fig- and pomegranate-shaded lanes behind the mosque, and almost swamped by undergrowth, it's still possible to visit the Hazana tomb, dedicated to a part-forgotten Jewish holy man of antiquity. Kamiran Islam, in his seventies, lives in a house directly across from the tomb.

"I remember very well, every Friday night the Jews came to pray here. I was a little boy. They asked us to light candles and gave us a coin or two," he told me.

Virtually all of Kurdistan's Jews left *en masse* to Israel in the early 1950s. Controversy persists as to whether they left voluntarily or were forced out, though in Amedi people freely acknowledge that their departure tore a hole in the social fabric that has never been repaired. Amedi's Jewish quarter today may be populated by Muslim and Christian families, but it retains its name and identity, and many townspeople offer a positive communal memory of intermingling.

"[Amedi's social mix] is lovely, it's one of the points that attracted me to study the city," says Dr Ismael. "But if no action is taken, Amedi will lose its value and significance, because the changes are so fast. Heritage is non-renewable: When you've lost it, it's gone."

Those changes are social—economic stagnation and lack of opportunity are driving younger generations away—but also physical. Heritage properties do survive, but walking today in the town there is plenty of evidence of new building, some of it unregulated. New residential neighborhoods have been established beside Sulav at the foot of Amedi's hill to cope with overspill, but as Wan Ibrahim, a postgraduate architect whose family can list seven generations of residence in Amedi, points out, many houses are vacation properties occupied only in summer, with absent owners. According to Dr Ismael's statistics, of every ten visitors to the area, nine stay in or near Sulav and never venture up the hill to engage with Amedi's long history at first hand. Dominating the hillside above Sulav is construction work for a $1.3-million hotel that will tip the scales yet further.

There's a sense of urgency to try and turn Amedi's fortunes around before it's too late. Alessandra Peruzzetto of WMF talks of a strong desire among the municipal and regional authorities, as well as the townspeople, to take action. Ismail Mustafa Rasheed, governor of Amedi district, talked to me of "strategies of movement" already under way to address conservation. Dr Ismael and her colleagues are working with WMF to identify specific clusters of surviving heritage houses and parts of the bazaar, focusing on analysis of materials, designs and typologies of windows, doors and archways, and bringing in local architects to sketch possible reconstructions.

There are proposals to continue excavation work at the Qubahan School, a part-ruined complex below Amedi's cliffs in the valley that was, for several centuries during the Bahdinan Emirate era, one of Kurdistan's leading scientific universities, linked with the great al-Azhar University in Cairo and attracting students from around the Muslim world.

Efforts are under way to identify local artisans in crafts, terracotta and—an Amedi speciality—the sesame-seed paste *tahini* who could contribute to a reshaping of the town's economy towards new markets.

For Najat Shaban Abdulla, elected in 2018 as member of the Kurdistan parliament for Amedi, the trend of vacationing in Sulav while ignoring Amedi is a "disaster". "Cultural heritage is part of the economy now. All the focus is on Amedi. I ran on a platform of reducing unemployment. Linking that with heritage conservation can create jobs for Amedi," she says.

Asking around in town produces mixed opinions. Khalid Khayat, a bank executive, welcomes the new energy. "Protecting our heritage is very important. But we need new buildings, new hotels and restaurants."

Halbin Ismael, the university librarian, is "very sad" that Amedi has lost its visual appeal to modern buildings, but says: "We don't want Amedi to become a museum—we grew up there, it's our city, how can we leave it?"

Yet college lecturer Halkawt Rajab Basso, the fourth generation of his family to live in Amedi, says he is ready to leave to make space for the city's surviving architectural heritage to be restored.

But he may not have to.

Part of Peruzzetto's brief at WMF is to brainstorm new approaches for Amedi. One possibility draws on experience from the Jordanian capital Amman, where older semi-abandoned urban townhouses were slowly restored piecemeal as new generations realised the appeal of living in heritage properties. WMF is opening conversations with developers in Amedi to discuss implementation of traditional building techniques, in an effort to enhance existing heritage and encourage adaptive reuse of buildings.

Another idea transplants the concept of an *albergo*

diffuso, or 'scattered hotel', from Italy, where abandoned mountain villages have been transformed into vacation hubs, with individual properties restored for lodging or tourist services.

But Peruzzetto is determined to keep gentrification at bay. "The idea is to try and generate a sustainable income in Amedi that is not disruptive of the heritage and existing ambience of the town," she says. "Tourism is not the first objective. Protection is the first objective."

Standing at sunset on the edge of Amedi's cliffs, with sawtooth mountains looming behind and mist clinging in the ravines all around, among the hundred generations who've stood on the same spot, the idea of protecting Amedi at this crucial turning-point seems the least we can do.

The writer thanks Laween Mhamad, Miran Dizayee and Birgit Ammann for their help in preparation of this article.

SAUDI ARABIA: THE HAPPY ONES

Wildlife conservation / 2012 / AramcoWorld

"**I** was ten years old—I'll never forget it."
Ahmed Boug gazes across a hazy desert view from the heights above Taif, in western Saudi Arabia, reminiscing.

"We'd set off for a camping vacation in Abha, up in the mountains. This was before there was even an asphalt road there. It was wilderness, high above the town. We slept early, but then at dawn my father woke us all in a panic. 'Monkeys!' he was shouting. 'Quick, get everything!' We grabbed what we could. There were about a hundred of them coming through. They stole fruit, food, anything. Later, we went down into the valley to retrieve our stuff—shoes and toys. It was all such a shock for me! That was what sparked my interest in these animals."

A child's interest became a professional's preoccupation. Today, as director of Saudi Arabia's National Wildlife Research Center, Ahmed Boug is a world authority on those backcountry raiders who so shocked him as a boy —hamadryas baboons.

Unlike olive, yellow, chacma and Guinea baboons, which are all found only in Africa, hamadryas baboons (*Papio hamadryas*) live on both shores of the Red Sea, ranging from Ethiopia, Eritrea and Somalia across to the semi-arid mountains of Yemen and Saudi Arabia. *Homo sapiens* aside, they are Arabia's only endemic primate.

Hamadryas need access to surface water, for drinking, and cliffs or rocky slopes that can serve as sleeping sites. In Saudi Arabia, where they number perhaps 350,000, these conditions prevail only in a narrow corridor along the Sarawat mountain range, north from the Yemeni border for roughly eight hundred kilometres parallel to the Red Sea coast. In the deserts east of the Sarawat there are cliffs but no water. On the Tihama coastal plain west of the Sarawat, there are water sources but no cliffs.

Boug's home city of Taif, perched 1,500 metres up in the Sarawat, is ideal—and the city has become famous for its baboons. Around the western outskirts in particular they can be seen in their hundreds cavorting across rocky slopes, or loitering near parks and recreation areas cajoling leftovers from amused picnickers.

Boug drove me out to al-Hada, seventeen kilometres northwest of Taif, where the Mecca-bound Highway 15 drops off the high escarpment in a series of precisely engineered hairpin turns. There were baboons quite literally dancing all over the road. In a pullout before an epic panorama across the desert, we watched as males and females, adults and infants, bounded over the rocks lining the shoulder, and over the four-lane highway itself. Directly beneath a large sign reading "DO NOT THROW

FOOD FOR THE ANIMALS", drivers were stopping to toss fruit, bread and leftovers out of their car windows, drawing screeching, somersaulting baboons onto car bonnets and roofs.

* * *

Hamadryas baboons are not lithe, slender tree-dwellers. They are short, stocky and powerful. A full-grown male can weigh as much as thirty kilos, sporting a silver mane that fluffs out to form a broad cape across his cheeks, shoulders and upper body, exaggerating what is already considerable size and strength. A long, squared-off muzzle conceals razor-sharp canine teeth up to five centimetres long. Narrow eyes dart about beneath prominent brow-ridges.

Females are half as big, their short, brown hair lacking the male's impressive mantle. And the males call the shots, too, corralling females around themselves in the polygynous building-block of baboon society, a "one-male unit" (OMU). As we watched the fluster of baboons on the highway shoulder, Boug was able to identify several OMUs, each alpha male controlling a variable number of females from two to seven or eight, plus infants. Two or three OMUs live and feed together as a clan. Two or three clans maintain close contact as a band, and several bands form a troop of a hundred or more individuals, travelling en masse from sleeping site to feeding site to resting site and back each day.

Order is maintained generally by consent, sometimes by force: it's not uncommon to see a male baboon hauling a female around by the tail, to stop her straying.

"He wants to mate whenever he can," Boug explained,

pointing out a male responding to a sexually receptive female displaying her back end, swollen and vividly coloured showing she is in heat. "And this," Boug added, pointing to another male shepherding a group of females, "is a unique behaviour for the baboon in Arabia, an adaptation to the more arid environment here. Herding your females takes less energy than fighting another male to win them back. Conservation of energy is a key priority." Despite his expertise, for much of the last three decades Boug has been working alone. Only a handful of papers have ever been published on the hamadryas populations in Arabia. As human understanding of the natural world developed over the last century, it's as if baboons got left behind. Swiss primatologist Hans Kummer—a pioneer of hamadryas research, who first worked on Ethiopian baboons in the 1960s—has put forward an intriguing theory as to why. Many mammals, he wrote, entice each other to mate beyond the range of human senses, mostly through smell. Baboons, though, like humans, are visual animals, which means their physical displays and sexual exuberance affect us too. What's worse is they appear to be half-dressed: the male's mantle covers his shoulders, but—like the female—he is naked from the waist down. To some observers, baboons are embarrassing.

Misplaced moral outrage, Kummer suggests, lies at the root of why monkeys in general have been described so disapprovingly throughout Western culture. Right up to the the middle of the last century, in literature, film and popular culture, monkeys were characterised negatively, as pushy, greedy, shameless, even lecherous.

But in ancient Egypt, hamadryas baboons were revered, despite not being indigenous to the country. By the New Kingdom period (around 1500 BCE) baboons were being imported for ritual purposes from Nubia, in the area of modern Sudan, and Punt, an unknown land assumed to be somewhere on the southern shores of the Red Sea. Their exact status in Egyptian religion is not clear, but it seems they were seen both as vessels for the gods to inhabit, and as proxy humans. Painted scenes show baboons building boats and taking part in harvesting, and baboons may have been mummified as part of a process of royal reincarnation.

Hamadryas were most commonly associated with Thoth, one of the most important of deities, the scribe of the gods and fount of knowledge, and—in Thoth's depiction as the ape A'an—also the god of equilibrium, seeking balance by weighing the deceased individual's heart against the motive force of the universe. Representations of hamadryas in ancient Egyptian art abound, both in painting and sculpture, most often worshipping the sun in a pose which, many authors have theorised, derives from a distinctive position adopted by male baboons while being groomed, head back, palms out and arms upraised to the sky.

Yet in Arab literary culture, although baboons are mentioned in the *hadith*, they are significantly absent from a rich poetic tradition which otherwise namechecks every kind of wild animal, from oryx and gazelles to hyenas and wolves. Ahmed Boug—a literary scholar and published poet himself—laughs as he delivers an explanation tantalisingly close to Kummer's.

"Baboons are neither beautiful to describe, nor good to eat," he told me. "So the poets ignored them."

* * *

It's not clear how baboons reached Arabia. As Hans Kummer wrote in his landmark book *In Quest of the Sacred Baboon* (1995): "It is a puzzling situation. The hamadryas must have originated on one side or the other [of the Red Sea]. As yet, we do not know which."

Other mammals present on both shores of the Red Sea differ substantially from one another. Oryx and leopards, for instance, both show marked physiological and behavioural variation between African and Arabian populations. *Papio hamadryas*, though, is essentially the same in Africa and Arabia. This implies a long period of isolation, in which the species evolved to its present form, followed by a relatively recent spread of population to fill the current range.

Kummer favoured an African origin, putting forward the intriguing idea that the baboons were transported across the sea by the ancient Egyptians, who are known to have worshipped the animals. Queen Hatshepsut is recorded as having sent out an expedition in around 1500 BCE to the "Land of Punt", presumably located somewhere in the Horn of Africa, which brought back live hamadryas baboons. Kummer suggests that at some point during the rise of maritime commerce on the Red Sea, baboons simply jumped ship, establishing pioneer colonies in the mountains above Arabia's Red Sea ports.

If Kummer is right, the African and Arabian populations of hamadryas would be genetically identical—but he was working from visual observation, before DNA testing was widely available.

It took over a decade for more light to be shed. Working in the laboratories of the King Khalid Wildlife Research Center outside Riyadh, a team under British geneticist Bruce Winney announced in 2004 that diversity in the mitochondrial DNA of Arabian baboons indicates colonisation of Arabia must have taken place earlier than twenty thousand years ago, long before the emergence of human civilisations.

The baboons, therefore, made the journey themselves. Did they migrate slowly northwards from Ethiopia into Egypt, traversing the Sinai desert to enter Arabia from the north? If so, populations at the northern edge of the hamadryas' current range would be genetically closer than those further south. But Dr Winney's analysis showed marked genetic diversity between samples taken in Eritrea and Taif, at the northern limit of distribution on both shores.

So scientists looked south. The Bab al-Mandab strait, separating Djibouti and Yemen at the mouth of the Red Sea, is only thirty kilometres wide. During periods of glaciation, when global sea levels dropped significantly, the strait would have formed a land bridge. This is known to have happened at several identifiable points over the last half-million years, leading Dr Winney and his team to conclude that baboons likely crossed from Africa to Arabia between 130,000 and 440,000 years ago.

Then primatologist Takayoshi Shotake of Kyoto University, working closely with Ahmed Boug in Taif, developed a new idea. At some point in the distant evolutionary past, he suggests, a common ancestor of the baboon crossed the Bab al-Mandab strait into Arabia. The hamadryas then evolved its distinctive characteristics in isolation over hundreds of thousands of years, before crossing back and repopulating the East African mountains. A specific genetic difference between African and Arabian hamadryas detected in recent analysis appears to bear this idea out.

Professor Shotake's work is still in preparation, and so remains in the realm of untested hypothesis, but it offers an intriguing possibility. Far from being an African baboon marooned on the "wrong" side of the sea, hamadryas might be Arabian.

* * *

One afternoon Ahmed Boug took me to Wadi Liya, on the south side of Taif, where all the elements of a baboon habitat unite. The valley is steep-sided, with rocky cliffs affording secure sleeping positions. Smaller wadis and springs nearby channel water into Wadi Liya, where a dam has created a lake of fresh water. And there is plenty to eat: as well as wild food, such as acacia fruit and the succulent roots of the prickly poppy (*Argemone mexicana*), every morning the baboons make the short walk over to Ruddaf Park, a local picnic area, where they raid the dumpsters and trash bins for human leftovers, gathering as much as possible before the park rangers arrive for work and chase them off.

The proximity of baboon populations to Saudi towns and cities—particularly Taif, the kingdom's top leisure tourism destination—is causing friction. Only around sixty-five percent of Saudi Arabia's baboon population is wild. The remainder is classified as "commensal", meaning they rely, to varying degrees, on human food.

"Commensalism has been a problem here for a long time," Boug told me. "But it's got worse in the last thirty years, as rapid development has overtaken environmental issues." Four percent of the baboon population—that is, several thousand individuals—are now completely reliant on human food sources.

But, as the drivers at al-Hada demonstrate, it's not just about raiding: the baboons are being fed. "In Islam," Boug explained, "some people think monkeys and pigs are people punished by God for disobeying divine law. They feed them to gain spiritual credit."

He told me about a local character, known for going around town filling sacks with leftovers from restaurants and bakeries, and taking it all out to al-Hada for the baboons. I drove to al-Shafa, a tourist area of fun parks and picnic grounds in the hills south of Taif, where visitors were buying fruit from roadside stalls and tossing it directly to waiting baboons.

I asked three young men, visiting from the coastal city of Yanbu, why they did it. "I don't know," said one. "I've never thought about it."

"It's a good thing to do, to get mercy from God," said another.

At one of al-Shafa's scenic overlooks, perched before a breathtaking panorama of forested crags and plunging ravines, Suleiman—weekending from the northern city of Hail with his friend Humaid—was setting up a barbecue.

"Feeding the baboons is part of praying and fasting," he told me. "It's a good thing to do. And they have nothing else to eat. If they had enough food they wouldn't come to us, would they?"

Such misguided intervention is having drastic consequences. In the wild a troop might total a hundred and twenty animals; commensal troops have been counted at more than eight hundred individuals. Yet with no need to search for food, they roam over much tighter areas— seven or eight square kilometres, compared with more than three times that in the wild.

The crowding that results is causing social breakdown. As males find themselves unable to keep order in oversized OMUs, "floating females" drift away to mate with unattached males, who, in turn, club together to seize more females. The tail-gripping behaviour in the commensal troop at al-Hada, where males physically restrain females, is stress-induced, and absent in the wild. Overfeeding is also shortening the interval between births, adding to the overcrowding. Baboons who eat discarded junk food that is high in salt, sugar and fat are showing health problems, including increased levels of intestinal parasites.

The problems spread wider still. With such close proximity, diseases such as bilharzia and tuberculosis are being transmitted to humans. Baboons are raiding farms around Taif, stealing crops and destroying infrastructure. One troop gained entry to an army base, ripping up seating in military vehicles and biting through radar cabling, causing two million riyals (US$500,000) of damage. Traffic accidents are increasing in the area, not just from animals on the highway: in 2010 Jeddah-based Arab News reported claims that a Taif man died when baboons threw rocks at his truck.

There are, says Ahmed Boug, simply too many baboons living too close to people. He is clear about why it is happening—a combination of habitat fragmentation, mainly through deforestation and overgrazing, and hunters killing the baboons' traditional predators, notably wolves, leopards, and hyenas.

Baboon behaviour may also be changing. In 2011 a video posted on YouTube of hamadryas baboons in Taif apparently kidnapping feral dogs to raise as pets went viral. At this writing [August 2012], it has had more than half a million views. The three-minute sequence, excerpted from a French TV series on animal behaviour, first shows a male baboon seizing a puppy by the tail, prodding it and dragging it along in the dust, then switches to a scene of adult dogs and baboons apparently relaxing together, as a narrator intones: "Kidnapped pups grow up with the baboon family, feeding with them and sleeping together." Mellow scenes of mutual grooming fade as the feel-good music swells.

Kidnapping has long been understood as a normal aspect of baboon behaviour. Males will attempt to seize infant baboons from nursing females as part of a strategy for improving their status within the troop. But why might a baboon kidnap another species? Overlooking its emotionally manipulative music and narration and carefully edited visuals, does this decontextualized video clip really show baboons seeking canine companions, and dogs responding to baboons as masters, or is this a case of humans projecting ourselves into the picture?

Symbiosis is familiar across the natural world. But pet-keeping—where one species adopts another for no obvious functional reason, taking responsibility for a lifetime of feeding and care—is virtually unknown. Outside captivity, only *Homo sapiens* is known to do it. Koko the gorilla famously kept a kitten, a Kenyan hippo befriended a giant tortoise, and there has been a handful of other cases, but they all occur in artificial environments. In the wild, chimpanzees in West Africa have been observed seizing hyraxes—small rodent-like mammals —for brief periods of play, but they invariably kill them shortly afterwards, in some cases for food.

For this reason, the clip drew the attention of Hal Herzog, a specialist on human-animal interaction at Western Carolina University. In columns for *Psychology Today*

and *Huffington Post* Herzog collated multiple viewpoints to explore the possibility that these baboons might be keeping dogs as pets, remaining sceptical while raising questions glossed over in the video:
– How long do the dogs live with the baboons? Is it long-term or temporary?
– Do the baboons get anything from the dogs other than somebody to love and play with? How do the dogs benefit?
– Do the baboons ever kill or eat puppies?
Answers, so far, remain elusive. John Wells, co-founder of the Saudi Arab American Baboon Research Association, a small volunteer organisation based in Jeddah, reacts in similar fashion. "I'm also sceptical," he told me. "I'd like to see the unedited footage."

Nonetheless Wells maintains that the video scenes are not unusual, explaining that he has observed baboons caring for cats. "In al-Shafa, I've watched as four female baboons came down a rocky slope to a mewing kitten. Straight away, the mewing stopped and the kitten rubbed up against them—it was playful behaviour, bouncing around. Then we saw the males come down the slope and take the kitten with them to drink."

In his book *Some We Love, Some We Hate, Some We Eat*, Herzog asserts that in order to have pet-keeping, you must have culture—that is, social imitation and peer approval. Is an abundance of food prompting Taif's commensal baboons to create "culture"? Are these animals, stuck in a stressful, overcrowded environment that is full of material benefits, keeping pets for comfort? For now, we can only guess—and Ahmed Boug is clear: his priorities are on practical steps to address commensalism and keep baboons wild.

In Abha in the late 1990s, the NWRC was able to reduce baboon numbers by half by gaining the support of regional and city governments to implement a two-pronged approach. Scientists used humane culling (similar to the methods vets use to euthanise pets) along with vasectomies and hormone implants to bring the birthrate down, while officials deployed public signage and promulgated local laws enabling police to issue fines for roadside feeding. Both elements—targeting human behaviour as well as baboon proliferation—are critical.

"If it's not done as one package, it won't succeed," Boug explains. "Just eliminating baboons is not a solution—other wild groups will move in and become commensal. We have to stop people feeding baboons. And the only way to do that is through public awareness campaigns."

To do this, the NWRC has funded environmental education in high schools and opened a new visitor centre. As this article goes to press [August 2012] Boug is organising a workshop to brief government officials in Taif on the issues surrounding baboon commensalism, identifying environmental causes and offering guidance on sustainable solutions. He is just back from a global primatology conference in Mexico, which showcased significant success in a long-running programme to control populations of macaques around Hong Kong through contraception and legislative intervention. Pending local government approval in Taif, Boug is ready to implement the same methods in Saudi Arabia. But it's a long, slow journey.

* * *

Back at al-Hada, vehicles are crowding the highway

shoulder, seven or eight in a line, their occupants coo-
ing as young baboons stuff their mouths with tossed-
out leftovers under the gaze of imperious, silver-caped
males watching from the rocks nearby. A lone municipal
worker in orange overalls collects discarded plastic bottles and food wrappings.

Appearances notwithstanding, none of this is new.
Merchants and travellers between Taif and Mecca have
passed through al-Hada since antiquity, and the old
stone road over the escarpment still exists beside the
highway. Medieval scholar Yaqut al-Hamawi described
al-Hada in his *Mu'jam al-Buldan* ("Dictionary of Countries") of 1228, drily noting the resident baboons. In
much the same vein, an internet search reveals plenty
of exasperated comments attached to videos of the baboons' antics. "I live in Taif," writes one Waleed Gilani.
"Every time we go to Mecca or Jeddah these baboons give
us a really tough time... sometimes we take a different
road..."

In formal Arabic, baboons are called *qurud*, connoting
misers or those who lives cheaply—derived from a word
meaning "unlucky". Yet in popular speech, most people
know them as *sa'dan*, "the happy ones".

But watching the baboons at al-Hada, filching scraps
from well-meaning drivers, with abundant springs close
at hand and the safety of the rocky cliffs as a night-time
retreat, their third name seems the most appropriate of
all—*rubah*, "those who profit".

SAUDI ARABIA: BY ANY OTHER NAME

Culture & society / 2011 / BBC

This short radio script, written from Saudi Arabia during the 2011 Arab uprisings, starts off as one thing and ends as another. The second half describes a very strange episode, which I didn't understand at the time, and still don't today, almost a decade later. The essence of it was I describe, but in order to protect the person involved—and with the approval of my BBC producer—I changed the context. The encounter did not take place in an airport, and it lasted for longer than I indicate. Had I described the setting faithfully, my interlocutor would have been easily identifiable to, say, the Saudi government, should it have wanted to identify him. Perhaps that wouldn't have mattered—indeed, the whole conversation was so outlandish it crossed my mind that perhaps this person was working for the Saudi government, engaged in some elaborate fishing expedition to test the responses of a visiting journalist to a provocative story—but that chance was not for me to take.

E ast of Mecca, Saudi Arabia's Highway 15 scoots across the sweltering Tihama plain. Switchbacks as tight as the coils of a desert viper climb two thousand metres to Jabal al-Hada, the Mountain of Tranquillity. Prophet Muhammad came this way 1,392 years ago, resting in the highland city of Taif and sampling the local grapes. Today, Taif is the focus of Saudi Arabia's multi-billion dollar domestic tourism industry. There are luxury hotels, holiday apartments and family picnic areas. But grapes have given way to horticulture. Since Ottoman times, farms all around Taif have cultivated the damask rose, a pink, thirty-petalled beauty.

At this time of year [April 2011], by sunrise Saleh al-Nimri is out in his fields with a team of workers, picking as many as forty thousand roses in a morning. "If we leave the rose until noon," he tells me, "all its perfume will evaporate." And that perfume of Arabia is indescribable —robust, spicy and dizzyingly complex. It is, almost literally, a world away from the clear simplicity of an English rose.

Every day during the spring harvest, lorries bring sackfuls of roses to factories all around Taif. Workers transfer the flowers to copper stills, each holding twenty thousand heads. Then the process of distillation begins. Sixty litres of fresh water is boiled down to forty of concentrated rose-water, which is then bottled for sale as a culinary and medicinal speciality. But the premium product is the slender film of rose oil left floating on top, which sells for an astonishing £25,000 a litre. It is only available in vials half the size of your finger. The scent of it knocks you sideways.

Shihab al-Qadhi, owner of Taif's biggest rose factory, tells me his grandfather began with one still. Now there are sixty. A small, precise man in middle-age, with neat silver beard and a brown robe, al-Qadhi shows me around, explaining the economics of the business and how he uses the petal residue after distillation for cattle feed. "It makes the milk taste rosy for weeks!" he grins.

* * *

A few days later in the airport departures lounge, still with the perfume of rose oil on my hands, I find an empty seat to wait for my flight. A few places along sits a businessman in red checked headcloth and sparkling white robe, creases neatly ironed.

After a minute or two he leans over and speaks to me in English. "They make these chairs deliberately uncomfortable, you know," he says. We get chatting. He says he is an accountant from a town in the north, returning after a company meeting. We talk about his work and then—cautiously—move on to politics.

In a low voice he tells me how one man in his local town had tried to launch a protest a couple of weeks before. It failed. The police had carted the man off to a psychiatric unit.

"But," says the accountant, "our media is not free. They didn't report any of it."

While we talk, there is a constant click from his wooden prayer beads. Muslim men across the Arab world and beyond carry prayer beads. Ostensibly they are a device for meditation: each bead, as it passes through the fingers, stands for one of the ninety-nine sacred names of God in Islam. But more often people toy with them absent-mindedly, even swinging them around carelessly on one finger while chatting on the phone. Nobody gives them a second glance.

The accountant smiles conspiratorially, leans over and shows me his prayer beads.

"If they saw this," he says, "I'd be in big trouble."

I look down. In his palm, nestled in the coil of beads, is a small silver crucifix. I goggle. He closes his fist, leans back and carries on playing with what I now realise is a Catholic rosary.

In Saudi Arabia, apostasy—that is, the rejection of Islam by a Muslim—carries the death penalty.

I look around. People are browsing the duty-free. Normal life carries on. Nobody noticed.

"I'm a Muslim, of course," says the accountant. "The beads are from my Christian lover in Beirut."

I boggle at him. Saudi law allows adulterers to be punished with death by stoning.

This man is carrying his personal protest with him in plain view. And he's chosen to reveal his act of rebellion to an audience of one in an airport lounge.

We spend perhaps another five minutes together. He tells me about his wife and kids, shows me a photo of his house—then he gets up, says goodbye, and goes off to catch his flight, briefcase in one hand, rosary in the other.

He never asked me my name. I never asked him his.

And everything smells of roses.

SAUDI ARABIA: A WADI RUNS THROUGH IT

Urban ecology / 2012 / AramcoWorld

Down by the lake, Hussein al-Doseri is beaming.
"Before all this there were no services here, no trails, no routes. Now it's easy."

An athletic thirty-something, in white T-shirt and huge wraparound sunglasses, al-Doseri stretches his arms wide to show me the landscape of trees and open water that forms Wadi Hanifah, shimmering in the unlikely setting of a dusty industrial suburb in south Riyadh.

For years treated as a dumping-ground and open sewer, the wadi has been the focus for a ten-year restoration project, which in November 2010 won the Aga Khan Award for Architecture. It has plenty of fans in the Saudi capital.

"I come here all the time, day and night," grins al-Doseri. "It makes me happy, to relax and spend time with my family by the water. It feels like the opposite of Riyadh. Nowadays, if I want to meet friends, I tell them: 'To the lake!'"

* * *

Rising in the highlands of al-Hissiyah, on the Najd plateau of central Saudi Arabia, Wadi Hanifah runs southeast for around a hundred and twenty kilometres before losing itself in the al-Sahbaa sands, on the fringes of the Empty Quarter. It drains a huge part of the eastern Najd. Fed by more than forty tributaries, this great watercourse has a catchment area covering more than 4,500 square kilometres across what was historically known as al-Yamamah.

Dry for most of the year, though fertile thanks to aquifers close to the surface replenished by seasonal flooding, the long, meandering valley ('wadi' in Arabic) has attracted human settlement for millennia. Centuries before the rise of Islam, a tribe known as the Banu Hanifah—their name derives from the Arabic word for 'pure' or 'upright'—were farming and trading between large, well-watered estates up and down the valley. Among the many cities they founded was one which became al-Yamamah's capital, known originally as Hajr ('Stone'). Described first-hand by the fourteenth-century traveller Ibn Battuta as "a beautiful, fertile city, with abundant water", it eventually gained the bucolic name by which it is known today: al-Riyadh ('The Gardens').

By the eighteenth century, Wadi Hanifah had taken on a role as a highway of ideas and conflicts. A 1744 agreement between Muhammad ibn Saud, the ruler of

Diriyyah, a town on Wadi Hanifah, and religious scholar Muhammad ibn Abdul Wahhab—from al-Uyayna ('The Little Spring'), in the wadi's upper reaches—established what later became known as the First Saudi State. The Saudi-Wahhabi alliance remains in force today. From a base at Diriyyah, Saudi forces conquered large parts of Arabia before military defeat in 1818. Diriyyah was abandoned and settlement shifted a short way downstream to Riyadh. When Abdulaziz ibn Saud finally secured Riyadh in 1902, it was the first in a chain of victories which led to the establishment of the modern Saudi kingdom in 1932, with Riyadh as its capital. Diriyyah was subsumed into the larger city, its nineteenth-century mud-walled ruins overlooking the wadi protected as a UNESCO World Heritage Site.

As a village, then a small town, Riyadh grew sustainably with its population. But from the early 1970s, as Abdullatif Al Asheikh, president of the Arriyadh Development Authority (ADA), has stated, "significant expansion in the city's area [and commercial activity] affected the wadi badly." Rapid growth quickly overwhelmed fragile ecosystems. Construction firms damaged Wadi Hanifah's landforms by quarrying for stone and extracting soil for building works, undercutting the flood channel's banks. There was unregulated mining for minerals. Date palm plantations flanking the wadi encroached dangerously into the flow channel, which was also blocked in places by uncontrolled dumping of domestic, commercial and even clinical waste. Seasonal flash floods swept pollutants into residential neighbourhoods and then left stagnant water in the wadi for months at a time, jeopardising public health.

By the 1980s demand was overwhelming Riyadh's

traditional approach to water usage, centred on conserving self-replenishing natural sources. Aquifers were being tapped ever deeper. The water table dropped beyond sustainable limits. To make up the shortfall the city turned to desalinated water, piped four hundred kilometres from the Gulf coast.

But sudden abundance caused its own problems, including surface runoff and rising groundwater contaminated with sewage, most of which was channelled into the already-choked Wadi Hanifah. Construction between 1975 and 1984 of the city's first (and, until 2007, only) wastewater treatment plant at Manfuha, beside the wadi in southern Riyadh, led to upwards of 400,000 cubic metres of poor-quality effluent being discharged into the wadi every day. Smelly, unsanitary water pooled into lakes downstream.

As local farmer Ibrahim al-Salim told the ADA: "There came a point when it was impossible for us to stay any longer. We left the valley."

* * *

Riyadh receives less than one hundred millimetres of rain each year. That amount tends to come all at once, in the form of sudden winter downpours. Only ten days a year on average, spread between January and April, have rain. The remaining eight months are completely dry.

Rain across the Najd desert, which surrounds Riyadh, flows naturally into wadis. Since the Najd tilts from the high ground of the al-Tuwaiq escarpment, northwest of Riyadh, southward and eastward towards the Gulf coast, all its wadis feed run-off water into the major artery of Wadi Hanifah, which is oriented towards the southeast.

With the distances involved, and the number of tributaries serving Wadi Hanifah, this means that by the time the Najd's post-storm waters reach the edge of Riyadh, they have grown into a potentially destructive flash flood. A key feature of the restoration project was to define the wadi's flood flow channel, then engineer grading and channelisation to control the flow on its path through the wadi.

Long-standing director of the ADA's Wadi Hanifah Restoration Project Saleh al-Fayzi spoke to me with passion about his involvement.

"I started working on Wadi Hanifah about twenty years ago," he said. "[At that time] it had a very bad reputation. It was the city's backyard dump."

In 2001 al-Fayzi headed up a wide-ranging ADA programme of restoration and redevelopment, which still continues. Working with Canadian firm Moriyama & Teshima Planners and UK-based engineers Buro Happold, the ADA has cleared garbage from the wadi, graded, landscaped, introduced flood-profiling measures, replanted native flora and devised innovative sustainable techniques to treat the city's polluted wastewater.

Walking in the wadi today, few signs remain of the ignominious recent past. At al-Elb, thirty-five kilometres north of downtown Riyadh, where high desert bluffs overlook a small dam, the western bank now hosts a line of carefully designed individual family picnic pods, backed by tall bankside palms. Each pod comprises a horseshoe of roughly finished pale limestone slabs, offering open views out across the wadi—which, here, holds water only in winter—while ensuring seclusion from passers-by. More slabs, laid horizontally, create steps and graded slopes down to the wadi bed, where children scamper along nature trails and extended families relax in the shade of the acacias. There is street-lighting along the pedestrian promenade beneath the palms, ample parking and a newly designed block holding public washrooms and toilets.

With a breath of wind at my back, and birdsong overhead, I talked to Saud al-Ajmi, civil engineer at the ADA.

"We have no open space in Riyadh," al-Ajmi explained, as we sat gazing out over the broad wadi bed to the bare tablelands atop the ridge. "No gardens, no beach. Wadi Hanifah has become a place to breathe."

In other big cities you might head up to high ground to gain a sense of perspective and a breath of air. In Riyadh, counter-intuitively, you head down. From al-Elb, for a full eighty kilometres south through the sprawl of Riyadh, Wadi Hanifah acts like a flue, drawing breezes over the city to relieve pollution and temper the heat. Move from city to wadi and, as well as a two- or three-degree drop in temperature, you instantly gain the calm familiar from a retreat into nature: concrete, traffic and skyscrapers yield to foliage, quiet, long views and—in parts —flowing water.

* * *

I took a drive with Christopher Walter, a landscape architect working with ADA. He explained how the road through Wadi Hanifah was formerly used as a crosstown short-cut, a narrow, dangerous route that was largely unmanaged. As part of the restoration project the road has been re-engineered deliberately to nudge through-traffic away. Speed bumps, circles and a forty kilometres per hour speed limit mean that the only traffic down in the wadi now is local.

We stopped near the point where Riyadh's Northern Ring Road—a perpetually busy multi-lane highway —crosses Wadi Hanifah on an overpass. Down below, birds chirped in what felt like a desert garden. The wadi was perhaps a hundred metres across, rounded limestone cliffs on either side peeking above high-walled date farms. Urban clamour could have been half a day, rather than half an hour, away.

"It's an oasis," Walter said.

We ambled down into the broad, dry flood channel, identifying the newly planted flora as we went— tamarisk trees, the yellow flowers of 'needle bush' (*Acacia farnesiana*, known in Arabic as *anber* or *futnah*), mature *Acacia tortilis* and *Acacia gerrardii*, fluffy fountain grass (*Pennisetum setaceum*), and many more. Each of the stone-bedded planting cells fills out the curves of a sinuous walking trail.

As al-Fayzi explained to me, the wadi has become a green corridor between the east and west of the city, easily reached from all points. It is open, without gates. Bilingual signage using a distinctive green and gold colour scheme is both prominent and consistent. Information boards show a satellite image of the wadi's full length divided into nine named zones, with interpretive text and a "You Are Here" marker, alongside icons for mosques, toilets, walking trails and other features. And every sign bears the project's logo, a stylised branch of *Acacia farnesiana* which identifies in a single glance that this is a place of nature, part of—but separate from—the city.

As we strolled Walter pointed out dense banks of silvery saltbush (*Atriplex halimus*) and boxthorn (*Lycium shawii*, also known as *Lycium arabicum*) to either side. "Shrubbery is absorbent," he said. "We deliberately overplanted, to let the wadi find its own natural balance. All these bushes will thin out in time. Overplanting also promotes seed propagation—it helps to populate the wadi with indigenous species."

I wondered why, in a valley full of date palm plantations, where the newly designed recreation areas feature avenues of palms, none had been planted in the wadi itself.

"Date palms can drink two hundred litres of water a day in summer," Walter said. "But if their root balls stay submerged, they die. The ones we planted here were failing because of high groundwater levels, so we've replaced them with water-tolerant *Dalbergia sissoo* [a variety of rosewood]."

Walter pointed out to me the trapezoidal DWFC, or Dry Weather Flow Channel, running down the centre of the wadi bed, formed by melon-sized chunks of local limestone. Both the shape and the material minimise erosion damage. He explained that side-roads crossing the wadi—such as to access farm property—have been lowered and the downstream side of the crossing packed with limestone rocks, gently sloped for ten metres to dissipate the power of the floodwater and minimize erosive sub-surface eddies. In a few places where landowners had encroached on the wadi, the ADA has resorted to compulsory purchase orders to widen the flood channel and, again, minimise the flow's destructive power.

* * *

As Wadi Hanifah approaches the edge of the city centre

its character changes. Beside the low-income neighbor-hood of al-Uraijah, a box culvert enters from the east bringing surface run-off from around the city. From this point on, the wadi holds a continuous flow—though, ini-tially, the water is untreated and still unsafe.

It's slightly further downstream at al-Utaiqah where the project's core idea, and its defining conceptual ele-gance, is revealed. Overlooked by ceaseless traffic on one of Riyadh's busiest highway interchanges, where King Fahd Road meets the Southern Ring Road, a new biore-mediation facility takes the city's run-off and transforms it—entirely naturally, without chemical or mechanical intervention—into water clean enough for irrigation and recreation.

Bioremediation, which means applying natural pro-cesses to repair environmental damage, refers here to the creation of a linked series of wetland habitats. Three large ponds, totalling nine hundred metres in length, their herringbone design clearly discernible on satel-lite mapping websites, host 134 bioremediation cells. Within each cell, algae and other aquatic and riparian plants form the basis of a food web, which—aided by de-sign features such as weirs and baffles—effectively filters the water, removing toxicants, harmful bacteria and other pollutants. Following bioremediation the wadi water, though non-potable, is clear, odourless, and safe for human contact.

The process is intricate. First, untreated run-off en-ters the bioremediation facility over a weir—which adds dissolved oxygen, killing coliform bacteria—into a main head pool, where suspended solids begin to set-tle. An aeration system (the only mechanical element of the process) adds more oxygen, then water enters each biocell across weirs into a two-metre-deep pool. There, micro-organisms flourish on specially designed submerged structures, feeding on organic matter in the water and themselves being consumed by tilapia fish. Within each cell the water then passes over a low weir into a wetland zone, about fifty centimetres deep, enclosing three small islands planted with trees and grasses to provide a riparian habitat alongside the aquatic environment. Contaminants in the water continue to be assimilated by micro-organisms and tilapia, with dragonflies and other insects, frogs, snails, aquatic molluscs such as clams, and birds also entering the food web.

The water then descends through a narrow riffle zone within each cell, lined with limestone baffles to aid oxygenation, before crossing another weir into an outlet channel serving the next head pool, for more aeration. Organic sediment decomposes (helped by more tilapia), and inorganic sediment settles, for flushing and dredging.

Over the entire nine-hundred-metre route, the bioremediation process functions with a precisely engineered gradient of just thirty centimetres. It currently treats 600,000 cubic metres of urban wastewater every day.

It's a startling process to observe, where dirty water enters and clean water departs, without any human intervention in between. Farms around the city are the chief beneficiaries, though plans are afoot to link a sustainable nursery growing replacement plants and trees for the wadi into the irrigation system. Fish caught in a fifteen-kilometre stretch—downstream to the point where effluent from the Manfuha plant enters—are edible. Indeed, restoration has spurred growth in fishing as a leisure activity.

Aquaculturist Eric Morales, who monitors the water

quality daily across twenty-two parameters, has been watching the facility become its own urban wildlife sanctuary. Recorded bird species include eagles, egrets, herons, and even seagulls, and Morales has spotted catfish and turtles in the head pools. The Saudi Wildlife Commission is launching a programme to study the new habitat.

None of the bioremediation techniques is new, but nowhere else have they been brought together on such a large scale, or at such dramatically reduced cost: bioremediation represents roughly one-third the capital outlay of traditional treatments. Now that the technology (or lack of it) has been shown to work in Riyadh, the next step is to explore its application in other, similarly challenging environments around the world.

* * *

One busy Friday at Stone Dam Park just south of the bioremediation facility, where clean water passes over weirs and through rock channels into a broad, scenic artificial lake, Egyptian Fathi Noor Hassan was sitting pensively in front of two rods as friends chatted all around and young children played under the palms.

"Before, I was afraid to come here with my family," he told me. "It was oppressive, too overgrown. Now,"—and he gave a little chuckle—"I feel like I'm by the Nile. If I get a break, I bring my kids down here to fish."

Further along the shore, I got talking with Saleh and Osama, two teenage friends grilling kebabs on a little barbecue. I asked them how they heard about Wadi Hanifah.

"There was something on TV," they said. "Then we noticed these signs." They gestured to the green and gold acacia logo on a location marker nearby. "The first time we came we thought it would be desert, but this is land-scaped. It's really different."

Stone Dam Park is typical: every weekend of the year, recreation zones up and down the wadi are crowded with visitors, as families and friends eat, play, and relax under shade trees beside the water. At the al-Masane Lake Park I found a cricket match in full swing, South Asian workers taking advantage of a patch of open ground.

In awarding the Aga Khan Award for Architecture, the 2010 jury stated: "The Wadi Hanifah project eloquently demonstrates an ecological way of urban development." Leisure and tourism are obvious winners from the restoration, but as project director al-Fayzi told me, property prices have had a boost, as individuals and developers seek new opportunities in previously shunned neighbourhoods. Restoring the natural balance has stimulated gentrification, with bankside landowners upgrading their perimeter landscaping to match the wadi's designed space.

More powerfully still, in a region where showy megaprojects so often display contextual disdain, it seems that this most ambitious of engineering schemes—reportedly costing the Saudi authorities around a billion dollars—has reconnected the city with a key aspect of its self-identity. Wadi Hanifah is where Riyadh was born, yet for years, in al-Fayzi's words, "nobody liked it". The wadi has shifted from being a source of shame to one of pride in less than a generation.

When London saw salmon returning to the cleaned-up River Thames in the 1980s, it was as if an old wrong had been righted. When a 2010 study announced that the

Potomac River had regained its beds of river grass, it was a step on the way to expunging the shame of LBJ's declaration that Washington's polluted waterway was "a national disgrace".

Riyadh has, likewise, regained a tangible linkage of culture and geography.

"We are just starting to bring high-school and university students, to establish a knowledge base in environmental education," Christopher Walter told me. "Water has completely changed this landscape. This is the first generation to deal with the wadi [in its restored state]. The story is not over yet."

KUWAIT: THE WITHOUT

Politics & society / 2013 / BBC

The tailor leaned forward, tweaked some wild rocket off the bunch, deftly rolled it together with cardamom-flavoured rice and shreds of lamb, then popped the bite-sized ball into his mouth.

"This government," he said, between chews, "they are fascists. Face like sheep, heart like a wolf."

In an airy tent pitched on the desert plains west of Kuwait City I'd been greeted by a circle of plump, middle-aged men. After coffee, dates and tea, the twelve of us squatted on the carpeted ground for lunch together.

The tailor, like the rest, was *bidoon*—short for *bidoon jinsiyya*, meaning "without nationality". Kuwaiti in culture, language and sensibility, he was nonetheless officially stateless, lacking citizenship or rights.

The story of the *bidoon* starts in the years around 1961, when Kuwait gained independence from Britain. Some people at that time came to be citizens while others did not—but exactly how remains unclear to this day. The issue rests on Kuwait's 1959 Nationality Act, which granted citizenship to those able to prove residential ties extending back before 1920. That included chiefly Kuwait's urban merchant class and ruling elite, but excluded many others. The government line is that some of those left out, lacking pre-1920 roots, tried to hoodwink officials into granting them citizenship by declaring false information. Others, the government says, simply chose not to take up citizenship.

The latter, at least, has the ring of truth. The concept of nationality was unfamiliar at the time, particularly for the semi-nomadic bedouin, who roamed without recourse to border authorities.

Later, amid a climate of suspicion during the Iran-Iraq War of the 1980s, Kuwait amended the Nationality Act to define the *bidoon* as "illegal residents", expelling many. Following the 1991 Gulf War, which ended Iraq's occupation of Kuwait, the *bidoon* who remained in the country found themselves accused of collaboration, sacked from government jobs and increasingly marginalised.

Today the *bidoon* number at least 106,000 people, though no reliable figures exist. They remain effectively barred from public education and most jobs, unable to get birth certificates or own property. The tailor at my desert lunch explained that he had to register his car and his business in the name of a Kuwaiti friend. Another man showed me a marriage document which gave his wife's nationality as "under investigation".

A government committee examines individual cases, but officials—like many Kuwaitis—assert that most or all of the *bidoon* are foreigners who have concealed their identity to gain the material benefits of Kuwaiti citizenship: free education, free healthcare, no taxes, subsidised housing, lavish unemployment benefit, a monthly food allowance, and more.

Rights campaigner Dr Rana al-Abdulrazzak, a director at Kuwait's Central Blood Bank, highlights the role of state-controlled media. "[People in Kuwait] neglected the *bidoon* issue because we couldn't see it," she told me. "It was never discussed."

She goes further, accusing the Sunni ruling elite of discriminating against the *bidoon*, many of whom are Shia. "We've been taught to be selfish: Kuwaitis are very racist," she said.

Such candour is rare, though most Kuwaitis nonetheless do shun the *bidoon*, either for sectarian reasons, or often through a sense of urban superiority.

In Kuwait City I met an architect from an elite family, who spoke to me on condition of anonymity. He told me: "The *bidoon* have no leverage, but they are in all senses Kuwaiti. Citizenship is their right." He declared an insignificant two-cent rise in fuel prices would cover the "negligible" cost of absorbing the *bidoon*, and described the situation as "shockingly inhuman".

"It is apartheid," he said.

I drove with *bidoon* activist Abdulhakeem al-Fadhli to Taima, on the outskirts of the capital. Tin-roofed shacks flanked an open drain, flowing along broken alleyways. A patch of waste ground, where *bidoon* rights' demonstrators regularly face down the security forces' tear gas and rubber bullets, has been defiantly renamed "Freedom Square".

At a *diwaniya*, or social gathering, in Taima, al-Fadhli explained his reliance on social media.

"The Arab Spring gave us the biggest motivation to believe we can do something," he said, emphasising that the *bidoon* were opposing the government, not Kuwait's monarch. "But," he added, "we know America will not come for us."

Since I met him [in November 2012] al-Fadhli has been re-arrested following a fresh round of protests, and is currently [January 2013] awaiting retrial following a two-year jail sentence imposed *in absentia*. Campaigners allege that he has been beaten and tortured while in police custody.

A constitutional monarchy with an elected parliament, Kuwait is generally freer than its Gulf neighbours. Yet having ignored the *bidoon* for so long, it must now deal with an entire disaffected generation, born in poverty, raised with little or no schooling and now self-educated in human rights.

As across the Arab world, the *status quo* appears increasingly untenable. Absorbing the *bidoon* into mainstream society would anger many Kuwaitis. But inaction could be costlier.

OMAN: IN SEARCH OF SINDBAD

Cultural heritage / 2008 / Gulf Life

Ali Juma al-Araimi rubbed his chin. "No, I don't know anything about Sindbad," he said, and leaned on the heavy teak door of his workshop, masts of replica miniature dhows rising behind his shoulder. "But ask on the shore around sunset. People might know."

It had been six months earlier, in a tourist guidebook to Oman, that I'd read: "Along with Sohar, it's been said that Sur was the home of the legendary sailor Sindbad."

In the West, Sindbad (or Sinbad) is a fairy story, the subject of swashbuckling movies for children. Visiting the home of Sindbad would be like making a pilgrimage to the birthplace of Indiana Jones. Yet Sindbad is a key character in the 1001 Nights, a merchant who, while seeking his fortune in the East, survives terrible dangers and battles outlandish monsters. How real could he be?

I started googling—and there he was again, on the Omani Ministry of Information website: "The legendary sailor Sindbad is thought to have originated in Sur." Virtually every site I found about Oman dropped in a line about Sindbad—but not one pursued the idea beyond recycling the claim.

Yet when I went back to the 1001 Nights, the text was unequivocal: "My father," Sindbad says, "was the chief merchant of this city [Baghdad]." Later, he adds: "I bought merchandise and set sail [from] Basra."

So Sindbad was Baghdadi. How, then, did the idea arise that Sindbad came from Oman? And was there any evidence for the claim, written or verbal? I asked Dionisius Agius, an expert on Arab seafaring traditions at Exeter University.

"There is no written evidence to back Oman's claim that Sindbad was Omani," he told me. "It is a genuine, lingering folk tale: coastal Arabs want to associate themselves with a legendary figure."

That piqued my curiosity even more. Was the story of Sindbad's voyages still being told? What kind of folk memory was being kept alive in Oman? I vowed to try and find out.

※ ※ ※

First stop was the Beit al-Baranda historical museum in the Omani capital, Muscat, a splendid old house set back from the Muttrah harbourfront. The director, Malik al-Hinai, explained how the tales of Sindbad probably originated in India, with the Sanskrit Panchatantra story cycle, and had become inextricably linked in popular imagination with the exploits of Ahmad bin Majid, an expert navigator who helped Portuguese explorer Vasco Da Gama discover the sea route from Africa to India in

1498.

But long before Ahmad bin Majid, al-Hinai added, Omanis had been famed for their maritime skill: in the ninth and tenth centuries, Sohar—just up the coast from Muscat—had been the largest port in Arabia, burgeoning on the back of links of trade and slavery established by Omani sailors with Baluchistan, Yemen and Zanzibar. Those maritime roots run deep. Thirty years ago, when Irish explorer Tim Severin arrived in Oman to re-create Sindbad's legendary voyage from Arabia to China, the old stories resurfaced. Severin worked with local crafts workers in Sur, a port south of Muscat, to build his ship according to traditional methods. The voyage was a success and the vessel, named Sohar, now resides atop a traffic roundabout on the edge of Muscat.

So, I asked al-Hinai, are there actually any links, literary or otherwise, between Oman and the Sindbad tales? His eyes twinkled.

"Omanis are famous for travelling, and Sindbad was a traveller," he said. "So let's have him as Omani!"

* * *

Sur sprawls across broad sandy beaches, almost at the easternmost tip of Arabia, its low, white façades peeling in the salty air. I stopped first at the dhow yards, ranged along one side of the lagoon—a natural harbour that safe-guarded Sur's position as a fulcrum for maritime trade. Keralan workers were busy carving, sawing and planing half-built replica dhows for the tourist trade.

But when I asked the boss, Ali Juma al-Araimi, about Sindbad, he knew nothing. Following his advice, at sunset I went down to the Fateh al-Khair, a full-size dhow mounted on the shore that is the last remnant of Sur's ocean-going fleet, once Oman's main link with Zanzibar. Lean, dark-skinned teenagers hurried past to join the twenty-a-side football match already under way on the beach. A group of middle-aged men sat out beneath a gazebo, eating ice cream and rolling chilled bottles of mineral water up and down their ankles. Everything smelled of the sea and hot sand. Nobody could tell me about Sindbad.

Masoud al-Mamiry, an Omani born and brought up in Zanzibar, gave a twisty smile when I asked him about Sindbad's origins. "Well," he grinned, "why shouldn't we claim him as Omani?"

Masoud and I roamed the town centre, crossing to al-Ayja, Sur's crumbling old quarter across the lagoon. There, on a back street, we found a little shop selling stationery and children's toys named Sindbad Sur Trading.

"People have come in before asking about Sindbad," harrumphed the owner. "But it's just the name of the shop." He looked away. "Kids see Sindbad in cartoons. They want to be like him."

❊ ❊ ❊

I left Sur to forget its past and headed up the coast to Sohar, the other Omani claimant to be birthplace of Sindbad—a port described in the tenth century as the wealthiest city in Oman, gateway to China. I walked the long, breezy Corniche, looking for any remnant of past glories, but there was nothing. Even Sohar's harbour was gone, long since silted up and built over. Only the pristine white fort remained, raised in the nineteenth century over an eighth-century predecessor. Three kids were kicking a football under the battlements. "Sindbad? Wasn't he Iraqi?" said one. He was spot on— but his mates laughed and threw the ball at him.

* * *

In Sohar's handicraft souk, Juma al-Hamdani, born in 1947 into an old Sohari family, shook his head. "There's nothing left," he said. "Sindbad was a real man, who lived in Sohar a thousand years ago, but all these stories have faded away. I'm proud of them; it's our history, but you can't sit with your grandchildren like you used to."

As he was speaking, a young Omani walked in to have his belt repaired. While the old man bustled away, I talked to the newcomer. "Sindbad?" he said, suppressing a laugh. "It's just a story."

I started back towards Muscat. On the highway, a few minutes outside Sohar, I suddenly noticed a roadsign pointing inland. SINDHA 13KM, it said. Sindha? It was worth a look.

A few breezeblock shacks nestled in the scrubby dunes. I stood in the fierce heat with Salem al-Badi, white stubble peppering his hollow cheeks, exchanging pleasantries, then feeling like an idiot for asking whether his village might perhaps have been named after Sindbad.

"Sindbad?"

He thought for a long while before responding.

"I don't know anything about this—and the people here who did know are all dead," he said. "If you want to find out, go and look for them in the sand."

And he lifted an arm, gesturing into the parched desert.

OMAN-UAE-SAUDI-JORDAN: CHILD OF BEAUTY

Wildlife conservation / 2009 / AramcoWorld

Out on the plains of central Oman, I watched the headlights of approaching vehicles coming at us across the Jiddat al-Harasis from maybe twenty kilometres away. A fingernail moon hung over the table-flat desert, shedding no light, as senior biologist Salah Said al-Mahdhoury and I were shown into the grand reception hall of one of the leaders of the Harasis people, Sheikh Muhammad bin Thamna al-Harsusi.

We rested on cushions, were shown the honour of being served dates and fresh fruit from the hand of the sheikh, ate from a huge communal platter of meat and rice, and talked late over spiced tea and unsweetened coffee about the Arabian oryx and its meaning to the Harasis.

"This is the original place for the oryx," the sheikh told us amid an animated discussion, as members of the sheikh's family and others chipped in amiably. The evening felt like a retelling of tribal knowledge accumulated over generations of following and admiring this iconic, antelope-like animal.

"It's not easy to hunt oryx—you can't chase them; they hide flat on the ground."

"They're like a military company: there's a ranking hierarchy."

"Oryx think like human beings in organising themselves: the leaders take shifts at the head of the herd."

One grizzled character spoke up. "Even if you've shot an oryx and it's down, if you approach, it will jump up." Heads nodded, and tales followed of hunters speared by half-dead oryx, followed by personal recipes for the date-and-butter poultice used by the Harasis to staunch bleeding.

As the tales wound on, I asked Sheikh Muhammad how he saw the future.

"The Harasis are caretakers—this is the meaning of the word," he said. "But despite all the promises, we cannot see the future, because the future is not in our hands."

❊ ❊ ❊

Surprisingly slight, weighing only around seventy kilos and standing barely more than one metre tall at the shoulder, Arabian oryx (*Oryx leucoryx*) are remarkably well suited to life in their desert range, which encompasses much of the Levant, Iraq, Saudi Arabia, most of the Gulf states and Yemen. Their white coat reflects the sun's rays, helping them to survive the extreme heat. In the wild they are able to survive without drinking water for months at a time, instead absorbing moisture from the plants they eat. They are not aggressive, living peaceably in small herds averaging ten or fifteen animals, and can detect rain—it is thought by smell alone—over vast distances: oryx have been recorded walking as much as a hundred kilometres in twenty-four hours.

These perceived qualities—stamina, toughness, loyalty, self-discipline—have long endeared the oryx to the desert-dwelling bedouin, also drawing the attention of poets down the centuries. The ninth-century Baghdadi poet Ali ibn al-Jahm wrote of the oryx's elegant, almond-shaped eyes in a famous work sometimes entitled *Ayoun al-Maha* (Eyes of the Oryx):

> *The eyes of the oryx between Rusafa and Jisr**
> *Spark desire from a place I know – and a place I don't;*
> *They restore old love to me, even though I did not forget,*
> *Yet they fuel my fire with more fire.*

(*Rusafa and Jisr refer to bridges across the Tigris in Baghdad, though they also have deeper metaphorical meanings linked to ideas of yearning or longing.)

Dr Ahmed Boug, director of Saudi Arabia's National Wildlife Research Center and also a published poet and essayist, showed me a poem by Zuhayr bin Abi Sulma from the sixth-century collection known as the Muallaqat, which includes a description of a female oryx successfully repulsing dogs and hunters, her eyes "ringed with kohl", her horns "smooth and sharp". Another, celebrated passage from the Muallaqat, by Imru al-Qays, evokes an erotic conquest: "She shows me a throat like the throat of an oryx, graceful when raised."

Zuhayr introduced the concept, much used by later

poets, of an oryx symbolising human dignity. In the classic story-within-a-story tradition, many poems tell of how a tribe in difficulty would send a poet to a neighbouring tribe, where he would be welcomed with comfort and refreshment before embarking on a long, dramatic account of an oryx hunt—often full of idealised language and symbolic meanings—which would end with the hunted oryx seeking sanctuary in a place of comfort and refreshment. "In this way," Boug explained to me, "a tribe could ask for help from their neighbours without actually having to ask."

This poetic air survives into contemporary Arab culture, where the standard word for oryx, *al-maha* (also a common girl's name), is supplemented by a host of flamboyant synonyms, including *al-wudaihi* ('the clear one'), *baqar al-wahsh* ('cow of the wilderness') and *ibn sola* ('child of beauty'). Countless businesses, from media consultancies in Kuwait to fuel retailers in Oman, use the name 'oryx' to associate themselves with qualities of dignity, fortitude and even a core Arab identity. In Qatar, the oryx has been declared the national animal: oryx adorn the tailfins of Qatar Airways planes, and the 2006 Doha Asian Games was promoted with a cartoon oryx named Orry.

The fascination filtered across to European culture, in which the Arabian oryx is a prime source of the myth of the unicorn. Shy, elusive, brilliant white, and often seen only at a great distance—when, in profile, its two horns seem to merge into one—it was picked out by the Greek philosopher Aristotle. "There are some [animals] that have but a single horn: the oryx, for instance," he wrote in the fourth century BCE.

The idea stuck. Often mixing elements from Classical

bestiaries with Arab hunting poetry, medieval European authors described courtly knights setting out to hunt the unicorn—a noble, high-status pursuit that matched the prestige attached to oryx-hunting in the early Islamic period. Where Arab authors wrote of exhausted oryx seeking sanctuary in natural refuges, European writers and artists depicted hunted unicorns resting their heads in the laps of maidens.

The *Peregrinatio in Terram Sanctam*, a 1486 account of a pilgrimage to the Holy Land by German cleric Bernhard von Breydenbach, reinforced the conflation of fact with fiction. It featured illustrations by Dutch artist Erhard Reuwich of local fauna, including a camel, a floppy-eared goat, a Nile crocodile and a unicorn, reportedly spotted "on September 20, 1483, standing on a hill near Mount Sinai". At that time, wild oryx would have been widespread in the deserts of the Levant.

The Bible also mentions a horned wild animal of great fortitude, named *reem* (or *re'em*) in Hebrew. Many commentators theorise that it may refer to the oryx: modern spoken Arabic uses the same word *reem* to mean gazelle, but dictionaries of literary Arabic give *reem* as 'white antelope'. The Authorised King James Version of the Bible, published in 1611, even renders *reem* as 'unicorn', further muddying the waters.

Yet, throughout, oryx remain deeply intertwined with desert folklore. At Wadi Rum in Jordan, I heard a Mowgli-like folktale about the Bani Issa tribe, told to me by Dakhilallah al-Zilabia, an old man in his eighties who remembered seeing wild oryx as a boy in Saudi Arabia. The tribal founder, Issa, was caught by the horns of an oryx. He was carried up onto the animal's head, where he lived for two years: when the oryx bent down to eat,

Issa ate too; when the oryx drank, Issa drank. When Issa finally slid off the oryx's horns, he had become like one of the herd: he lived alongside the oryx, and would run off when people came close. "To this day," Dakhilallah said, "the Bani Issa will neither hunt oryx nor eat oryx."

Ahmed Boug, scientist and poet, has a unique vision for exploiting this powerful cultural heritage. "Culture and the arts are very strong tools to carry the message of conservation to the people," he told me. "I hope that reintroducing the oryx to the wild will also reintroduce them to the culture."

* * *

Since the last wild oryx was shot in Oman in 1972, that country has taken a leading role in global attempts to save the species, launching an initiative in 1979 to reintroduce oryx to the wild.

The focus for this project was the Jiddat al-Harasis, a stony, semi-arid plain of karst limestone covering much of central Oman, named for the formerly nomadic Harasis tribe who live there. Oryx were bred and released into the Jiddat al-Harasis's Arabian Oryx Sanctuary—a vast, unfenced area which, at 27,500 square kilometres, was roughly equivalent in size to the entire country of Belgium.

By 1996, two years after being named a UNESCO World Heritage Site, the sanctuary hosted more than 450 free-roaming oryx. The project was universally deemed a success.

Yet as Dr Mohammed Shobrak, a conservation expert at Taif University and consultant to Saudi Arabia's National Commission for Wildlife Conservation and Development (NCWCD), pointed out to me, "Most of the countries starting out on reintroductions have the big picture. It's all about conservation, bringing animals back to the wild—but they don't have a detailed plan in place for what they're actually going to do. So you start to see problems developing after a few years."

From a distance, it is perhaps too easy to see how the Omani authorities' singling out of one tribe—the Harasis—to act as guardians, rangers and guides might have been likely to raise hackles among neighbouring, less favoured communities, notably the Janaba, pastoralists and fisherfolk who occupy the coastal lands to the east.

Unscrupulous animal collectors throughout the Gulf spotted the rift in tribal relations, and used money to widen it. From 1996 onwards, substantial sums were offered to the Janaba for live oryx—five thousand US dollars for a male, twenty thousand for a female. Oman's long, mostly unguarded international borders represented no deterrent, and insufficient resources exacerbated the oryx's vulnerability. According to biologist Yasser Hamdan al-Kharousi, in 2005 the sanctuary was operating with just eight rangers. Two four-man patrols were each responsible for guarding an area the size of Connecticut.

In less than a decade, Oman's oryx herds were decimated. Some animals died from injuries or stress suffered during capture, others were found dead having been dumped in the desert, limbs trussed, by fleeing poachers. Many, though, were taken and sold alive, either to vanish into private menageries or to reappear in public collections in neighbouring countries.

By 2007 there were just sixty-five oryx left, including only four females. That year a royal decree reduced the size of the Arabian Oryx Sanctuary by ninety percent, to 2,824 square kilometres. In response, UNESCO removed the sanctuary from its list of World Heritage Sites, [then] the only such delisting in the history of the organisation. The international press lambasted Oman, but the view from within the country was different. As Dr Andrew Spalton, Adviser for Conservation of the Environment at the Diwan of the Royal Court, and a world authority on the oryx, told me, "Oman chose to take the site off the UNESCO list. The oryx project was born into a country that has developed very, very quickly. Maybe it was ahead of its time. There is talk of the population of central Oman going from two thousand to two hundred thousand. These changes are huge, and the concept of having oryx in the wild has not kept up."

Later that year, virtually all Oman's surviving oryx were gathered into a fenced enclosure of just four square kilometres, where they remain today. They are protected by the Royal Oman Police, who patrol in four-wheel-drive vehicles, armed with automatic weapons. Yet the challenges continue. Since demand from collectors has declined, I learned that poachers have begun diversifying. Wealthy customers will now pay a thousand dollars for a kilogramme of oryx meat—and, despite all the safeguards, rangers are finding increasing numbers of butchered carcasses.

The fenceless Jiddat al-Harasis has simply proved impossible to police. The new sanctuary, soon to be fenced, is smaller, but still has around forty oryx roaming free across a sizeable area, equivalent to four times the size of Bahrain. Oman has admitted defeat—yet has also shown its determination not to give up on the oryx.

"In one or two generations we could try again," Dr

Spalton told me. "The rangelands are still viable. We didn't lose the oryx through disease: all our issues are socio-economic. If I could do this again, I would place much heavier emphasis on the balance of communities." With that in mind, conservationists across the region are urgently re-examining their approach, particularly to fostering supportive relations with local people.

I asked Dr Robbie Robinson, director of the King Khalid Wildlife Research Centre, north of Riyadh, to sum up the state of oryx reintroduction in Saudi Arabia. "It's good," he said, picking his words with care. "There's a population in the Empty Quarter, at Uruq Bani Maarid, with another large group in the Mahazat as-Sayd protected area. One is completely self-sustaining in an unfenced reserve, the other is burgeoning in a fenced reserve."

I asked how one might be able to judge a 'successful' programme.

"As a biologist," Dr Robinson said, "I would say that you have to have a population which is self-maintaining and which is in balance with its environment. Then there's a broader conservation element: are the oryx safe? In other words, is the population integrated into local community life, so you don't need high-intensity policing? Uruq Bani Maarid counts as very successful [on both counts]."

* * *

Uruq Bani Maarid is entrancing. Located about eight hundred kilometres south of Riyadh, this immense tract of wilderness—frequently abbreviated to 'UBM' (I even heard Arabic-speakers refer to it as '*yoobiyem*')—lies at the western fringe of the Empty Quarter. Vast longitudinal dunes of the softest ochre, overlying a plateau of Jurassic limestone, contrast with semi-arid gravel plains, nurturing flora and fauna as diverse as anywhere in this part of Arabia.

Walking among the *panicum* grasses and the *sarh* trees (*Maerua crassifolia*), conservation specialist Abdulrahman Khoja told me there were three hundred oryx living freely in the wild amid UBM's 12,000 square kilometres. Sixty rangers share daily patrolling duties. Despite remaining open and unfenced, UBM has suffered just twenty cases of poaching since 1995.

"We have very good relations with the people around," nodded chief ranger Muhammad bin Moajib.

Nearby in al-Mendefen village, Sheikh Mirbih bin Hadi al-Arjani welcomed us with sweet dates, fresh camel's milk and ginger-spiced coffee.

"I remember seeing wild oryx before the hunting parties started driving through here," he said. "When UBM [was set up], we were fearful that the government was going to take our lands away from us, but now we understand the concept of what is being done. We are delighted to see the oryx back!"

Sheikh Muhammad bin Abdelrahman al-Fahad, head of the Sultana region, told me: "The oryx feels like the prodigal son returning; it is part of the wealth of our community." In Khaldiya village, Sheikh Misfir bin Huwaysh al-Abdan didn't believe the oryx would ever return, but is now "so proud to have this animal back". North of UBM, farmer Saud bin Khalaf ad-Doseri thanked God for the opportunity he'd had, as an old man, to finally see wild oryx for himself. The enthusiasm spanned boundaries of age, clan and tribe, as if everybody felt a part of the success.

This pride was tempered with a strong message of contempt. In Sheikh Mirbih's words: "The person who is weak inside, who doesn't understand the oryx—he is the hunter." Sheikh Muhammad went further: "Nobody hunts unless he's crazy or stupid or bad-mannered." In truth, I couldn't tell how much of this sentiment was heartfelt, and how much delivered to this visiting journalist in the knowledge it is what external authorities want to hear.

Hunting has been outlawed by governments from Oman to Jordan, but enforcement remains patchy—and with hunting deeply embedded within rural culture, it's questionable whether banning the practice is the most effective long-term strategy for conserving the oryx. Robbie Robinson calls such legislation misguided. "It might have been more profitable to educate hunters, to try to integrate hunting into conservation," he told me.

Othman Abd ar-Rahman Llewellyn, an environmental planner with Saudi Arabia's National Commission for Wildlife Conservation and Development, and a specialist on Islamic approaches to conservation, agrees.

"By working with the hunters we could develop a new ethic," he said, pointing out that the sixteenth-century jurist Ibn Nujaym established a principle of Islamic law which states: "Hunting is permissible, except for sport." As Llewellyn has written, "At what point does the hunter's legitimate pleasure in his tracking skills, or the excitement of the chase, become sport?" He defines it as "a matter of intent", and suggests that religiously sanctioned trophy hunting could be used as a means to generate funds for wildlife conservation.

This last idea reflects a shifting emphasis worldwide, as conservationists try to build bridges of social inclusion. Older methods of pouring resources into protecting 'flagship' species at all costs (the panda, the tiger and so on) are giving way to favouring conservation of habitats, thereby ensuring that hundreds of species survive together—and that rural communities remain viable.

These issues are felt acutely in Jordan, which has spotlit oryx conservation for more than thirty years, yet has never been able to conduct a successful oryx release. Overgrazing by sheep and goats has destroyed desert habitats—and, with them, any chance that the oryx could survive in the wild.

In 2005 Jordan's Royal Society for the Conservation of Nature (RSCN) changed tack, downplaying the oryx and instead starting to work directly with local communities on broader environmental projects, incorporating perhaps the most powerful device by which this newly inclusive, habitat-focused conservation can gain exposure (and, therefore, resources): nature-based tourism. Yet despite many successes, Jordan's pioneering work is being outpaced by grand schemes under way in the United Arab Emirates.

Abu Dhabi's Environment Agency recently began reintroducing oryx to Umm az-Zumul, a remote desert zone three hundred kilometres south of the oasis city of al-Ain, comprising almost 9,000 square kilometres of gravel plains backed by immense sand dunes. Ninety-eight oryx were released there in 2007. About the same number are due for release in 2009, with more to follow.

"A lot of zoos around the world breed animals with no goal," Mark Craig, director of al-Ain Zoo, the largest in the Middle East, told me. "But we have one oryx population on display, and another 'back-of-house', maintained specifically for reintroduction. They have a different diet, closer to what they'd get in the wild—less protein, less availability of water."

I asked Craig if the aims of Abu Dhabi's oryx reintroduction project were purely conservation, or whether there was a commercial element. "There'll be a bit of both," he said. "It's just for the animals, but there will be a strategy of ecotourism as well."

That strategy centres on two luxury resorts created by Abu Dhabi's Tourism Development and Investment Company (TDIC). The 'Desert Islands' project, launched in late 2008, focuses on a modestly sized wildlife park of thirty-five square kilometres on Sir Bani Yas island, holding four hundred Arabian oryx alongside fauna from giraffes to dugongs. An opulent five-star hotel offers game drives and leisure activities.

Meanwhile Qasr al-Sarab ('Palace of the Mirage'), another luxury hotel, is under construction alongside Umm az-Zumul. Due for opening in late 2009, it will feature oryx safaris among attractions from saunas to stargazing. I met wildlife officer Ahmed Abdulla al-Dahaeri nearby for the long drive to the oryx release zone.

We passed through magnificent scenery at the eastern fringes of the Empty Quarter, dunes piled in every shade of apricot and ochre, divided by immense plains of *sabkha* (salt flats). At one point al-Dahaeri turned to me and grinned. "It's beautiful," he said. "We released gazelle here eight or ten years ago. Now it's the turn of the oryx."

Umm az-Zumul is vast. During a couple of days there, the only time I saw the fence was as we entered, and as we left. The Environment Agency has gone so far as to plant an entire forest of *arrak* 'toothbrush' trees (*Salvadora persica*) at Qisseiwara, in the deep desert about twenty-five kilometres in from the Saudi and Omani borders, to provide food and shade for the oryx—essential in an area recording highs of 62C. Nearby, I saw a herd of sixty or seventy gazelle—from a total population topping three thousand—grazing on irrigated lawns in the wilderness. I watched rangers dropping alfalfa for roaming oryx, and feeding bottled milk to abandoned oryx calves. Al-Dahaeri showed me an artificial lake, on the shores of which the Environment Agency has built a solar-powered filtration plant, converting saline groundwater into drinking water for the animals.

Conservation projects around the world frequently struggle—or fail—to find sufficient funding. Yet in the UAE, if the project suits, money appears to be available in almost limitless quantities. Now that there is also a boom in Gulf tourism, the oryx have suddenly gained new currency: they have become a tool for business. This conjunction of wildlife reintroduction schemes with world-class tourism development neatly demonstrates one route to a sustainable future for the oryx in Arabia.

I put this to Mubarak al-Muhairi, managing director of the TDIC and director-general of Abu Dhabi's Tourism Authority. "The oryx are an attraction," he agreed. "When we picked the location of Qasr al-Sarab, we coordinated with the Environment Agency. We wanted them to bring the oryx to that area [Umm az-Zumul]. In the future, visitors will not notice that this is a managed programme."

✻ ✻ ✻

To test that notion, I detoured to the al-Maha Desert Resort, in neighbouring Dubai emirate. Al-Maha (the Arabic word for oryx) sits within the Dubai Desert Conservation Reserve (DDCR), and has won numerous tourism awards for its sensitivity of design and its conservation ethic.

The hotel comprises a main building housing reception and restaurants, with guest chalets spreading to either side across the lightly wooded dunes, all offering magnificent, elevated views over the desert. The DDCR's conservation manager Greg Simkins told me: "The Arabian oryx was part of what we wanted to do—getting people who are visiting Dubai to come out and see an iconic animal that should be part of this landscape."

In that, they have succeeded with some style. Oryx meander, as if tame, across the paved paths between chalets, munching at the foliage as electric golf carts ferry guests to and fro. On a nature drive I saw more oryx in one place than anywhere else—herds of twenty or thirty animals skittering over the dunes, their horns crisscrossing together against the sky.

Simkins is proud of the achievement. "It started with the resort, but the conservation side grew as we saw a bigger need for it. Serious conservationists now say this [profit-based] model could be utilised in different parts of the world."

In November 2008 the International Union for the Conservation of Nature (IUCN) agreed, granting the DDCR Protected Area status—the only example in the Middle East, and perhaps the world, of a conservation scheme of global scientific value emerging from a profit-oriented tourism project.

As a luxury packaged experience, al-Maha is unbeatable. Yet its commodification of the oryx is sometimes hard to swallow. Though the habitat was natural, the animals' behaviour clearly was not. This tourist, for one, did notice that the oryx were being managed.

* * *

Does giving humans a close encounter with wild animals merit trapping those animals and distorting their behaviour? This question applies to oryx in Arabia as much it does to tigers in Rajasthan, dolphins in Florida, or any zoo in the world. There is no easy answer. Almost everywhere, fences have proved to be a necessary evil. But then, for tourism purposes at least, fenced areas as vast as Umm az-Zumul's 9,000 square kilometres could legitimately be called 'wild'. The DDCR, at 225 square kilometres, is more problematic—though, as Andrew Spalton commented, "Can people differentiate between oryx in the wild and oryx behind a fence? That's not clear in my mind."

Yet "free-ranging" is a key point in international guidelines on reintroduction. When the oryx smell rain, they move towards it. A barrier will, sooner or later, thwart their natural instincts. "Mahazat as-Sayd, even though it's 2,244 square kilometres, is clearly not big enough," Robbie Robinson told me. "You get a number of years when there's no rain anywhere in there, so the oryx try to migrate and get stopped by the fence."

And a central issue that remains so far unaddressed by any of the tourism projects in the Gulf is the dislocation between the Arabian oryx and the Arabian people. When I visited the DDCR, I was greeted by Indian guest relations staff, led by South African guides, and served at dinner by Kenyan and Canadian waiting staff. Neither the resort nor the reserve employs a single Emirati.

Showcasing oryx in isolation from Arab culture impoverishes the tourist experience. But it also threatens to leave unaltered the cultural disconnect between urbanised populations and the roots of desert life—a widening fissure which, arguably, was to blame for the near-extinction of the oryx in the first place, less than forty years ago.

* * *

Jordan, to its credit, is attempting to tread a more culturally inclusive path. In 2008 its semi-autonomous Aqaba Special Economic Zone Authority (ASEZA) launched a partnership with Abu Dhabi to release oryx into the wild at Wadi Rum, one of Jordan's most popular tourist attractions for its natural beauty and links with Lawrence of Arabia. Abu Dhabi will be supplying sixty head of oryx, in three batches of twenty—the first is due to arrive as this article goes to press [September 2009].

Significantly, ASEZA is embracing the Dubai model of conservation-through-profit. Yehya Khaled, director of Jordan's RSCN, gives a hard-headed analysis: "The Bedouin will hunt the oryx to sell if we release without their ownership and support. And if we try to release in Jafr [a remote desert site far from tourist routes], the oryx will be lost, as in Oman. But in Wadi Rum it's easy to create ownership: the people see the oryx as an asset. Keeping an oryx alive will bring them more income than if they kill it or sell it."

This was borne out by my time in Wadi Rum: everybody I spoke to supported the project—not least because almost all of Rum's twelve hundred people gain their living from tourism. ASEZA environmental consultant Mahmoud Bdour explained: "Economic benefits are the tool by which we can reintroduce the oryx. We are focused on how to engage the local people with conservation of the place."

Yet despite admirable intentions, the Wadi Rum project seems fundamentally flawed. In Abu Dhabi, conservationists identified oryx habitats, then developers set about creating attractions. They have, in a sense, brought tourists to the oryx. Jordan, though, is trying to bring oryx to the tourists, by shoehorning a reintroduction project into an attraction which specialists doubt represents a suitable habitat.

When I raised the point with Khalid Irani, the Jordanian minister of environment, he gave a wry smile. "I'm usually an optimistic person," he said, "but I don't think this programme will fulfil its purpose."

* * *

As many as sixty million American bison once roamed the plains of North America. Uncontrolled hunting in the nineteenth century reduced their numbers to a few hundred individuals. From 1889 captive breeding and reintroduction—along with a change in hunting patterns—allowed the species to regain a foothold. Today, there are more than 300,000 bison in North America. Some areas have recently begun issuing permits for bison hunting in order to maintain a balanced population, while bison are now also widely raised for meat.

The return of the bison has many parallels for Arabia and the oryx. The days of free-ranging bison herds have clearly gone for good, yet it has still been possible to restore the animal to its native habitat—with all the romance and natural drama that connotes—within a new economic framework of ranching (that is, breeding the animals for slaughter) and controlled hunting. A similar shift in approach could be the way to redirect oryx conservation in the Middle East. With international cooperation, it's not difficult to conceive of a network of oryx reserves operating in tandem across several countries. Ranch-style reserves would breed oryx for hunters to pursue legally under permit control; educational reserves would showcase oryx and other native flora and fauna for students; tourist reserves would allow visitors to experience Arabian culture and wildlife in a semi-natural setting; and so on. What seems to be required is a recognition that merely saving the oryx from extinction has not been enough.

The oryx's survival has been assured; now what are we going to do with it?

✳ ✳ ✳

Out in the sands of Uruq Bani Maarid, walking among the acacia and *ziziphus*, it struck me that, despite all the mistakes, the oryx have a bright future. Thanks to the tourism projects in Abu Dhabi and Dubai, which boast good rangeland, lots of space, conservation expertise and generous funding, more people than ever before will have the chance to experience the oryx at close quarters. Expanding public education programmes at wildlife centres in Jordan, al-Ain, Taif and elsewhere will foster an ever-greater understanding about the place of the oryx within desert ecosystems.

Yet the most hopeful sign, paradoxically, is the failure in Oman. Since 2007 all misty-eyed optimism surrounding oryx reintroduction has evaporated. Successful breeding has been shown to be insufficient. The catastrophe on the Jiddat al-Harasis demonstrates, unequivocally, that social inclusion is vital.

UBM remains the one project which ticks all the boxes. As Robbie Robinson confided: "Coming from South Africa, where tourism is essential for conservation, I'm very pleased to be in Saudi Arabia, where tourism isn't essential for the oryx, and where there is governmental willingness to fund protected areas like Uruq Bani Maarid."

The baton for creating free-ranging, sustainable and well-managed oryx herds has passed into Saudi hands. Hopes rest on UBM.

OMAN: SATAN STAYS AWAY

Travel / 2012 / The Times

Salim's round eyes watched me.

"Satan only likes dirty places," he nodded. "He waits in toilets and rubbish bins. But if he smells this—" Salim grabbed a ceramic frankincense burner and wafted clouds of resinous white smoke under my nose— "Satan stays away."

Omanis take smell seriously. Arrive in Muscat and the first thing you notice is a lingering, seductive fragrance. Traditional ankle-length dishdasha robes, worn by men throughout the Gulf, in Oman feature a unique aromatic accessory: a dangling tassel, woven into the collar, that is dipped daily into scented oil. Omanis drift about in a cloud of their own sweetness.

But these are not the blended whiffs of commercial perfumiers. Souks and malls overflow with natural products that smell lovely. Visitors invariably latch onto culinary spices, but for locals the aromatics matter far more. Splinters of *oud*, a resinous wood imported from

Cambodia, sell at wildly inflated prices for burning in the home. *Bukhoor*, woodchips soaked in aromatic oils, are equally popular.

The daddy of them all is *lubban*, or frankincense, golden pearls of resin that, when burned, smell so heavenly Satan himself, it seems, dare not approach. In the bewitchingly smoky souk of Oman's second city, Salalah, frankincense vendor Salim wafted more devilproof fumes my way. A little bit peaches, a little bit furniture, it smelled to me like ancient history.

Gold remains as valuable as it was when three wise men visited that Bethlehem manger. Myrrh, a crystalline resin used in embalming, has lost its mystical power, now sold in Middle East bazaars for pennies as a child's decongestant. But frankincense still defines a nation. I sought its source.

A thousand kilometres from Muscat, southern Oman's Dhofar region is where the scraggly tree *Boswellia sacra* thrives. Its sap is frankincense, harvested by painstakingly scraping away bark, then returning days later to pick off the globules of hardened resin. Heated over embers to release the smoke, it has been central to religious ritual across the Mediterranean world for millennia. Ancient Rome imported vast quantities of the stuff thanks to a complicated supply network that led back, via camel caravan routes across the desert, to the sole, far-distant origin—Dhofar.

I spent days meandering around the low-rise Dhofari capital Salalah, watching shadows lengthen across whitewashed arches (the city's name derives from a local word for "white") and sipping sweet water from freshly opened coconuts, sold at roadside stalls beneath towering palm groves. Beside the excellent frankincense museum, packed with detail on maritime history, I dropped into Basma Alnobe's shop, selling frankincense oil, frankincense water, even frankincense soap. Men may harvest the resin, she smiled, "but it takes a woman to judge quality." The Queen of Sheba would agree. Her local palace lay just east of Salalah, by the coastal creek of Khor Rori. At the shadeless ruins of Sumhuram, above the creek, I looked down into the long galleries where frankincense would have been stored before being shipped to Yemen and up the Red Sea. It is said that Nero burned an entire year's supply at the funeral of his second wife, Poppaea, in 65 CE. I tried—and failed—to imagine the quantities involved.

Two hours north of Salalah, over the mountains that ring the coastal plain and into the sandy deserts beyond, the scanty ruins of Ubar lay mute beside scorched noticeboards. This former frankincense trading city was destroyed roughly 1,500 years ago in a cataclysm so huge it merited retelling in the Quran. It seems a giant sinkhole opened up without warning, swallowing the city— and memory of its location. Ubar was only rediscovered in 1992 using satellite tracking by a team led by Sir Ranulph Fiennes, and today remains far off the beaten track, a whistle-stop site on the edge of an immense desert.

I sat for a while with community elder Bakheit bin Abdullah, who dug with Fiennes. "We've already lost many things," he told me. "Life is good, but tourism is coming. I fear for the future here."

I reassured him as best I could. In terms of Western tourism, Salalah isn't even a blip on the radar. Oman Air runs shuttles from Muscat and Dubai, and Qatar Airways launches Doha flights next May, but that's hardly a stampede. Weekly charters from Stockholm and Helsinki deposit a few blinking Scandinavians onto the beaches each winter, and occasional cruise ships use the deepwater port as a stop-off between the Red Sea and the Gulf, but for nine months of the year Salalah slumbers.

That changes every summer, when the Indian Ocean monsoon brushes past. From June to September, while the rest of Arabia bakes, rain drizzles onto Salalah from grey skies, fog envelops the beaches and temperatures plummet to a balmy 20C. Saudis, Kuwaitis, Bahrainis and Emiratis pack into Salalah in their thousands: every soggy mountain meadow hosts an extended family, delightedly picnicking in the rain. The desert they have at home. Wet green grass makes a holiday.

Yet dodge the monsoon to visit in quiet October, as I did, and you experience scenery like no other in Arabia, under crystal-clear skies washed blue and luminous by the summer rains. The greenery persists: it could almost be England's Peak District, these rolling uplands cut by scrubby folded valleys—until you spot camels silhouetted on the ridge-tops.

"First we had frankincense, then we found oil," one insightful young Dhofari told me. "The next generation's wealth will come in solar power—but we will always love frankincense."

That passion crosses cultures. When Shakespeare wanted an image to counter the stink of corruption, he had a distraught Lady Macbeth mutter, "All the perfumes of Arabia will not sweeten this little hand."

But Shakespeare had never been to Salalah. They've got just the thing for her there.

OMAN: WIND AND SPIDERS

Politics & society / 2012 / BBC

I woke to the roar of total silence. Issa, an Omani bed-ouin of the al-Maashani tribe, made tea as the orange-lit theatrics of sunrise began behind us. It was just him, me and the soundless dunes of the Empty Quarter.

Dinner had been Issa's too—chopped camel meat fried in camel fat, chewy and delicious, washed down with ginger tea. Afterwards, we'd chit-chatted companion-ably in the dark, staring upwards as the Milky Way slid across a pinprick sky like the arch above Wembley Sta-dium.

We were camped in what the explorer Sir Ranulph Fiennes had called "a place of wind and spiders". In his day its name was Fasad, or "Decay". The spot had since been euphemistically renamed al-Hashman, mean-ing "Wholesome"—but with its broken walls and foully undrinkable spring water, that struck me as an oddly mirthless piece of spin.

There's a lot of that in Oman these days, as the country paddles ever harder to maintain its trademark swan-like serenity. The Arab Spring has come knocking. Last month a local journalist was jailed, accused of slander—the most high-profile of, so far, forty-two court cases related to issues of public protest.

Like most of its neighbours, Oman saw street protests last year and earlier this year—though protesters were calling mainly for salary increases and lower living costs, rather than revolutionary overthrow. The result, unusually, was a flurry of reforms. Oman's autocratic ruler, Sultan Qaboos, created tens of thousands of new government jobs, raised the minimum wage and introduced cost of living allowances for public sector workers.

He also reshuffled his cabinet three times in twelve months, purging unpopular ministers.

This nimble response took the wind out of protesters' sails. In the southern port city of Salalah, a local business leader chuckled. "What the people wanted, they got," he told me. "There's nothing to protest about anymore."

But not everyone agrees. Omanis I talked to expressed concern that the sultan's populist initiatives are merely an attempt to postpone genuine structural reforms. They might keep people quiet for five years, even ten—but then what?

And like the failed dictators of Egypt, Libya and Syria, Qaboos has personally identified himself with the Omani state. He is childless but has named no heir. It is illegal to insult him, but what counts as an insult is open to interpretation.

A man who told me, "Sultan Qaboos is thinking like it's the 1980s," refused—perhaps wisely—to give me his name.

Over ice-cream sundaes in Salalah, I talked with Abdullah al-Amiri, a systems analyst.

"Change is already affecting this country in healthy ways," he said. "But it is going very slowly." For Abdullah one key marker is social media. From desert herders to fashionable young students, almost everyone you meet is on Facebook, Twitter, WhatsApp, or all three.

The ubiquity of social media, and the impossibility of controlling them, is causing panic. The government has been busy all summer prosecuting and jailing dozens of online activists.

Yet the red lines aren't fixed. Instead, it's all about self-censorship. Lawyer Riyadh al-Balushi told me the law is deliberately kept ambiguous. "The barriers to freedom of expression are not legal," he said. "They are internal."

Oman's coastal capital Muscat lines up like sugar cubes on a narrow shelf. It is seductively calm: holidaymakers and Western expats move from villas and malls to the glittering new opera house freely, without hindrance.

But wait at the coffeeshops after dark to talk to some of Muscat's bloggers and tweeters, and a different picture emerges, of tell-tale clicks on the line during phone conversations, of unusual activity on Facebook pages.

One prolific Twitter user, a young Omani woman in a headscarf, gives me an old-fashioned look. "Of course the government is reading my tweets," she says.

The country's most popular political website is *Sabla*, a chatroom allowed to operate as a safety valve. Omanis joke that the first thing new ministers do is log onto *Sabla* to see what people are saying about them.

As a local journalist explained, the authorities will

generally let whatever is said in English pass. But they care deeply about what is said in Arabic—to the point of jailing dissenters.

Yet showing one face to the neighbours and another to the world is a strategy that rings hollow for Oman's globally connected youth, who are easily able to join the dots for themselves.

It seems only a matter of time before Omanis start using social media to hold the government to account.

As one young Omani told me, "Everyone loves Sultan Qaboos—but older people love him more."

With the monarch about to turn 72, but almost three-quarters of his population under the age of 25, Oman's generation game is coming to a head.

JORDAN: TO THE HOLY MOUNTAIN

Travel / 2013 / National Geographic Traveller

Even now, weeks later, I'm not sure why I cried. The tears were flowing before I reached the summit: I remember looking up into the blurry blue. I also remember, further back down the trail, when the old, familiar voices started to sing to me about weakness and tiredness and failure—but even then I knew I'd already beaten them. This time I was going to make it. I remember pouring water into my hat and jamming it back on my head. I remember chocolate. I remember the last few steps—steep ones, cut through rock, with a white dome floating above, glimpsed through salty lashes.

It was a place out of reach. A place I'd been looking at for twenty years but had never visited. It was high on the mountain-top, and it was deep down inside myself.

So I cried for the views. I cried for my own achievement. I cried for the holy ground I stood on. I cried for my

five-year-old son, who wanted to come with me because
he thinks all mountains are white and climbing one to
play snowballs with his dad would have been the best
game ever. I cried because there was no snow. I cried because I was crying.

In truth, I didn't want to come down. It was renewal.
Sitting there, shaded, looking east, I'd unwittingly become a pilgrim.

* * *

My journey to the mountain took almost three years.
Back in 2010 I realised an anniversary was approaching
for Petra, the two-thousand-year-old trading capital of
the Nabatean people that is now Jordan's top tourist attraction. I'd been to Petra maybe twenty times, over almost as many years. I'd been there at sunrise, at noon and
after dark. I'd studied it, walked it, watched it, hated it
and loved it. But the more I revisited, the less I knew it.

After its antique heyday Petra had lain undiscovered
for centuries. Baybars, a Mamluk sultan, passed through
in 1276, noting in his diary "most marvellous caves, the
façades sculptured into the very rock face."

But for five hundred years after Baybars—nothing.
Knowledge of Petra's whereabouts faded from outside
memory. The locals, of course, knew exactly where it
was, but they weren't telling. At that time, the moun-
tainous country between Damascus and the Red Sea was
virtually impenetrable to outsiders. Wild, lawless and
largely uninhabited, it lay beyond the reach of any government. There were few roads. Only a scattering of isolated settlements broke the rolling landscapes of stony
hills and semi-arid plains that led into the vastnesses of

the Arabian interior. Few, if any, travellers got through.

It was in that context that Swiss explorer Jean-Louis Burckhardt travelled. A man of extraordinary resourcefulness, Burckhardt had been hired in 1809 by the Association for Promoting the Discovery of the Interior Parts of Africa to find the source of the River Niger. His plan —to get to Cairo, and from there join a caravan bound for the Sahara—hinged on disguising himself as a Muslim: Christians and other outsiders without protection would have been prey for bandits. Burckhardt adopted the persona of "Sheikh Ibrahim", a merchant.

After two years in Syria, perfecting his Arabic and studying Quranic law, 27-year-old "Sheikh Ibrahim" set off for Cairo, keeping his meticulously updated journal hidden beneath flowing robes. On 22nd August 1812, crossing rough hills, he wrote: "I was desirous of visiting Wadi Musa [the Valley of Moses], of the antiquities of which I had heard the country people speak in terms of great admiration."

Burckhardt, at that stage, had no idea that Wadi Musa —which lay well off his path—held the ruins of Petra. Moreover, it was a dangerous detour. "A person like myself," he wrote, "without any papers to show who I was, or why I had taken that circuitous route, would have looked very suspicious. I therefore pretended to have made a vow to slaughter a goat in honour of Haroun [Aaron, Moses's brother and a venerated prophet in Islam], whose tomb I knew was situated at the extremity of the valley. By this stratagem I thought that I should have the means of seeing the valley on my way to the tomb."

It was a great idea. By playing the Haroun card Burckhardt was able to talk his way past tribal lookouts.

Below Wadi Musa his guide led him into a canyon lined with carvings, and on through an ancient city—which Burckhardt describes in close detail, later identifying it as Petra—before reaching the foot of Aaron's mountain. By then it was already sunset, and too dark to make the climb: they sacrificed a goat in sight of the tomb on the summit and turned back.

Burckhardt eventually made it to Cairo, staying five years, but in 1817, shortly before his desert caravan was due to depart, he contracted dysentery and died. His diaries, published posthumously, sparked a worldwide resurgence of interest in Petra which continues to this day.

What a life. What an adventure. And the two-hundredth anniversary of his epic discovery was approaching.

I hatched a plan. I was going to walk the same route, down the slopes into Petra then over to Mount Aaron (Jabal Haroun in Arabic)—but then do what Burckhardt could not: I was going to climb the mountain.

* * *

According to the Old Testament, the Israelites passed through southern Jordan after their forty years of wandering in the wilderness. Aaron died there, and Petra's highest peak, soaring to 1,330 metres, has long been associated with him.

A millennium later the Nabateans, builders of Petra, who carved shrines to their gods on summits all round the region, cut a stepped processional way up the holy mountain. Ruins of a Byzantine monastery dedicated to Aaron stand on a col near the top. Legend has it that the

Prophet Muhammad climbed the peak as a young boy, travelling with his uncle.

In 1338, the ruling sultan had a new shrine to Haroun built on the mountain-top, replacing a pre-existing chapel. The current incarnation—a modest one-room rectangular building, which dates from a 1495 restoration—is clearly visible from all round Petra, high against the sky. Its whitewashed walls are the first to catch the rays of the rising sun. Its low dome crowns Petra's jagged horizon every evening in silhouette.

Wherever you go in Petra, Haroun is in constant view —but few make the effort to approach him. I laid plans. It would be an event. There would be donkeys. Camels. Friends jostled to join the trip. I knew August would be too hot—Burckhardt was made of tougher stuff—so I fixed a date in cooler February. Emails were sent. Deals done.

Then erratic 21st-century weather patterns intervened. A week before the big day, Jordanian forecasters predicted a cold front, with plunging temperatures and heavy rain. I called everyone I knew. Teeth were sucked. Voices warned of capricious conditions, out in the canyons.

I arrived into bitter cold: who thinks to pack gloves for Jordan? Hoteliers stayed huddled by gas heaters. Guides were stamping feet and cupping hands round lit cigarettes, snorting smoky steam. Snow blocked the high-altitude roads. Thick skies hid Haroun. I cancelled the camels.

All that summer Haroun filled my mind. On anniversary day, 22nd August 2012, I gave a talk about Burckhardt at the Royal Geographical Society in London, and showed pictures of the mountain. It was becoming an obsession.

But something inside me had changed. Respect had grown, and a jolly jamboree now seemed wrong. The mountain, too, had grown. Was I biting off more than I could chew? I pondered going alone, so that I could fail in private. But then I worried about losing the way.

I sent some dates to Yamaan Safady, one of Jordan's best guides. He climbs mountains—almost literally—every day of the week. He'd probably been up Jabal Haroun a dozen times; it would be a stroll in the park, the slowest walk he'd ever done. Would he be willing? Of course, he said, and we arranged to meet on the first day of December.

By seven in the morning, we were alone amongst the canyons. Rather than follow Burckhardt's route, Yamaan had proposed a back trail he knew, approaching Petra from the north. We drove to the trailhead through silver streets, cockerels competing with the tinkling neckbells of goats.

Then distractions faded as we started walking beneath a mackerel sky that pointed arrows to the mountain.

* * *

"I wonder why those bedouin haven't moved down to the desert yet."

Yamaan had spotted a black tent, pitched some distance away. His voice danced for a while between cliffs before vanishing into the ravine.

"Maybe they're planting winter wheat. Then they'll move," he murmured.

There was a juniper tree—a young one, said Yamaan, only four or five hundred years old—and we paused on an outcrop for water and dried apricots. Buttery sunlight melted down the canyon's pitted old face. Mesmeric views went past the sandstone ridges, bent on their igneous black foundations, an unfathomable thousand metres down to the desert floor and beyond, out to the Holy Land.

Past a ledge above a chasm—hug the cliff, ordered Yamaan, and feel for the way with your feet—the going became sandy. I stumbled over bulbs of sea squill, sprouting at the foot of a rocky climb.

"Goats hate them too," grinned Yamaan. "But crested porcupines dig up one or two. I met some hunters a couple of weeks ago; they said they caught a porcupine as big as a lamb. Look!"

He broke off as an orange flash darted across the cliff-framed sky.

"Tristram's grackle! Shiny black, but the male has orange patches on his wing."

When Burckhardt hired a guide for the walk to Jabal Haroun, he paid him with a pair of old horseshoes. Burckhardt, you see, didn't have Yamaan.

I thought I spied a cairn, silhouetted ahead. Then my jaw fell. As we approached, I realised it was the immense, stone-carved urn atop Petra's largest façade, the Monastery. In twenty years I'd never seen the building from this angle. Wider and taller than the west front of Westminster Abbey, it was—like most of Petra—carved from solid rock two thousand years ago. Perhaps a royal tomb, or a gathering-place for religious ceremonies, though never a monastery, it defies scale. The doorway alone is taller than a house; the urn I saw towers fifty metres above the ground.

The Monastery is the furthest and highest that most

tourists go in Petra. As we descended the main access route—comprising about 750 rock-cut steps—threads of trudgers were puffing their way up.

We came down into Petra from the back, crossing the central Colonnaded Street beside temples, tent cafés and loitering camels. The hubbub was like a service station on the motorway: brief, a little dizzying. It was a relief to walk through and re-establish the rhythm of our journey.

* * *

Beyond the Amud Faraoun, a lone column standing on the slopes, we encountered no more tourists. Views opened across undulating country, with the white shrine of Haroun always visible on its distant peak as we skirted the titanic cliffs of Umm al-Biyara, heading south out of Petra.

Past the Snake Monument, a huge block carved by the ancient Nabateans as a coiled serpent, the path descended into Wadi Sabra, vast, sunny and silent. It led us around to approach Jabal Haroun from the shadeless southwest. I'd been walking seven hours, and could now hear the voices of tiredness and defeat.

Everything was about putting feet in front of feet. Yamaan saw and walked ahead, letting me fight my own fights. There was no climbing, or even scrambling. It was just an uphill walk, partly on steps cut by the Nabateans. But it was, somehow, the hardest thing I've ever done. Crystal sunlight poured from translucent skies. One switchback revealed views over the back of the mountain into unimaginably deep canyons, guarded by a single, luminous juniper. There was purity.

Near the top I heard a high, cracked voice. "This way!"

it said. "I've been watching you the last two hours."

After brewing us the sweetest, hottest tea at her shack by the fenced-in ruins of the Byzantine monastery, perched on a plateau below the final summit, brown-toothed Tamam wiped her hands on her old black dress, adjusted her headscarf, popped the key of Haroun's tomb into a pocket and led us to the last few steps. We were going to meet a saint.

The whole Burckhardt anniversary, which had driven me onwards since the beginning, meant nothing now. He'd climbed his own mountains. This was me, climbing mine.

✳ ✳ ✳

Back at home, a friend nodded when I told her I cried at the top.

"Some places do that to you," she said.

That reminded me of what Rosalyn Maqsood wrote, in her excellent book on Petra:

"*Believers accept that certain localities can be impregnated with the life-giving force of some saint or hero. Traces of their essential virtue would cling to their mortal leavings even though their spirits had passed to another world, and [would] be continually renewed by the constant stream of prayer and devotion emanating from the pilgrims who found their way there. These places are visited to gain healing, or fertility, or protection against dangers, or whatever is the desire of the heart. Jabal Haroun is such a place.*"

It is.

JORDAN: A VINE ROMANCE

Culture / 2009 / CNN Traveller

In an undistinguished commercial district of Amman, off one of the narrow streets that winds between the Jordanian capital's towering hills, I reach for the spittoon. But it's too late. The Sauvignon Gris —light, fresh, delicious—has already transported me far away to English Cotswold villages, somehow evoking on my tongue the ancient crumble of sunlit walls of golden limestone. I know I should spit. But it's too good.

"Limestone," I mutter. "Cotswold limestone."

In the armchair opposite, Omar Zumot, Jordanian entrepreneur and winemaker, frowns and takes another sip, sucking in air and slooshing the butter-coloured wine around his mouth. Then he beams.

"Amazing. I remember we planted these over in the corner, where the basalt yields to limestone. You're right. Amazing."

Wine-tasting, as Zumot says, is poetry. As his country's premier winemaker, he is on a self-declared mission to put Jordanian wine on the map, but it is often a struggle. Fifteen years after single-handedly creating Jordan's first commercial vineyards, and with a respectable range of high-quality wines to his name, Zumot still faces a wall of ignorance—and even mockery—from the wine establishment.

A 2007 story by the news agency AFP epitomises the stance, discussing Arab wine in terms of "Chateau Migraine". Omar Zumot isn't laughing. "This is my greatest concern," he says, "the reputation of Jordanian wine."

Jordan is one of a handful of Middle Eastern wine producers claiming Biblical origins for their wine industries. After a gap of more than a millennium, production restarted in the nineteenth century in Lebanon and Palestine, both influenced by French expertise. With consumption of alcohol forbidden to Muslims, their separate industries were developed in Lebanon by Christians, and in Palestine (and, later, Israel) by Jews. Both countries now dominate the region's winemaking, Lebanon producing around 150,000 hectolitres annually and Israel almost 60,000.

By contrast, according to figures from the US Wine Institute, Jordan makes around 5,000 hectolitres. Annual consumption totals under 0.1 litres per capita – compared with 1.1 in Israel or 3.5 in Lebanon. Zumot's 'Grands Vins de Jordanie' brand leads the way with its premium Saint George range, recognised as leagues ahead of the Mount Nebo table whites produced by Eagle, part of the local Haddad group.

Yet for a nation that is ninety-five percent Muslim to have a wine industry at all tells its own story. In Zumot's words: "Jordan is an Islamic country where you can make wine: how much more tolerant could you get?"

He takes me to his vineyard at Sama as-Sarhan, north-east of Amman on the Syrian border. This is frontier land —dry, bleak and windblown. To the east yawns an open wilderness of stony desert, while to the north looms the bulk of Jabal Druze, an extinct volcano that, at some point in antiquity, spewed fields of basaltic lava over this landscape. It is a most unlikely place to see vineyards.

"This is the last parcel of pre-desert land," Zumot says. "We chose it partly for the soil—it's basalt. While digging I noticed a new layer every half-metre. I thought it would be good to bring a mineral flavour to the Pinot Grigio and Sauvignon Blanc grapes, and we've had amazing results."

As we stroll between the vines, Zumot, 43, explains his background. Born in Amman into an old Christian family from Jerusalem—his father, Bulos, founded the Zumot company in 1954—Omar started training in accountancy at fourteen. In 1988 he spotted a gap in the market and began exporting gin and *arak* (an aniseed spirit) to Iraq, and made his first million within a year. When the Iraqi market crashed under sanctions in the mid-1990s, he launched a foodstuffs enterprise, chiefly importing and distributing potato crisps, which remains the mainstay of his business. But he has returned to his first love.

"I always wanted to be involved with wine. At nineteen I went to France to study winemaking at a monastery in the Ardèche, but I was young and stupid, and I spent years procrastinating. Then, in 1996, I started planting."

I ask what his philosophy is on winemaking.

"You can't make money selling wine in Jordan," he says. "This is not a business; it's my passion. And I try not to intervene as much as possible. My whole operation is fertiliser-free and pesticide-free. I was advised to spray against grape worm, but the birds take the worms for me. They charge me—we lose fifteen percent of the grapes to the birds—but this is nature."

He shows me a large fishpond. "I irrigate from here. It's fed by a renewable aquifer from under the mountain, and the carp manure adds nitrate to the water. I allow sheep into the vineyards to trim dead shoots from the Merlot vines: they eat the weeds, fertilise the soil and their saliva disinfects the vine trunks. My secret is really to produce as little as possible from each vine. We are yielding less than two tonnes of grapes per hectare [compared to a world average of 8.5]."

His gentle approach appears to be working. The company produces almost 300,000 bottles a year and is beginning to get noticed, with Swiss organic certification and multiple gold medals at the prestigious Mundus Vini wine awards in Germany. The American International Wine Review praised Zumot's 2007 Saint George Reserve Shiraz as "a delicious wine that holds its own against international benchmarks".

"The local market likes these butt-kicking wines," Harun Dursun, sommelier and manager at Amman's Grand Hyatt hotel, told me. "They want them full-bodied, powerful and fruity, with lots of tannins, to go with the pronounced flavours of the food. We get very good feedback, and justifiably so: in my opinion the Saint George is above average globally—and regionally it is top."

I settle in with Zumot for an extended tasting at his city-centre Winemaker outlet, which doubles as retail shopfront, warehouse and lounge. A uniformed assistant serves plate after plate of crusty bread, prosciutto and soft cheeses, while I make the acquaintance of that limestone-rich Sauvignon Gris and its cousins—a mineral-tinged Tocai, a vibrant Chardonnay, and more. Then we start in on the reds.

Zumot beams again, pushing up his glasses like an excited schoolboy and pouring from a bottle of Shiraz Grenache. I take a sloosh, and let the high, sweet fumes fill my nose. Something hidden refuses to show itself.

"This is a promise, not a wine," he remarks. "We don't crush these grapes: we just de-stem them before pressing. And we let sedimentation occur naturally in oak barrels, handmade by Chassin in Burgundy. It needs another couple of years."

The afternoon winds on, encompassing a bold Carmenere Cabernet blend ("Forgive the tannins," says Zumot), superb Merlots and, unexpectedly, a delicious Graciano, culminating in the resonant, characterful Pinot Noir Winemaker's Selection, which won gold in Germany. Neither of us troubles the spittoon much.

At the splendid old restaurant Haret al-Jdoudna ('Courtyard of our Forefathers') in Madaba, a historic market town southwest of Amman, the maître d' greets Zumot warmly. We are shown to a quiet corner, and our table is crowded with mezze – an array of salads, bite-sized pastries, dips both hot and cold, grilled meats and freshly baked flat bread, designed to delight the eye and nose as much as the stomach.

Zumot gestures around, at the packed restaurant. "It's not only the freedom," he says. "We have the culture. I love my country!"

JORDAN: A DESERT MEMOIR

Travel / 2014 / Beacon

C heek to the dust.
Blow.
Face away to breathe.
Blow again.

The call to prayer begins down below, from the one-room mosque by the tree in the valley. But as usual with children, the reality of the moment has overtaken us. The call to prayer doesn't matter. What I thought was the point of coming here has been shown not to be so.

The smoke makes me blink. Woody. I can taste it as I breathe, to blow. It reminds me of times in tents, staring into embers while pinching handles of hot tea glasses, and of the aromatic woodsmoke that still clings to a plastic rainjacket I brought here once, to Jordan.

I love that jacket, for the way it smells.

Cheek to the dust again.

Blow.

Suleiman leans in to blow, too.

* * *

You have an ancient name, Isaac. "He who laughs"—that's what it means, in the odd, biblical way that doesn't look like it could possibly make sense. Your mother chose it. Your mother is very wise. I think she understood you before you were born. You laugh, my son. You laugh a great deal.

* * *

We came here, to Feynan, because I wanted to show my kids the desert.

When I was eleven, somewhere south of Jerusalem, my dad stopped the car; I don't remember why. I was already walled in by adolescent confusion and expectation. It was a long drive, in a strange holiday.

I opened the back door and got out; I don't remember why. Through the layers of created memory I can, though, still recall the shock of the desert. It was big, bigger than I could understand. Folded mountains. My mum, the day before, or the day after, said the desert looked like a rumpled tablecloth. I remember not understanding that. It looked like mountains to me. I don't think I was adult enough to hold mountains and dining room in my head at the same time.

My mum and dad—they're indoors people, with tablecloths. I didn't know that then, but it made me see the desert mountains as they did, as TV, as unrelated to my inner self.

The sun was inexplicably hot. It had never been that hot before.

And then my dad turned off the engine. Maybe I asked him to.

Utterly silent. The light. The emptiness. Quiet. Implacably unreadable, the landscape. Not that I realised I couldn't read it, an eleven-year-old boy from English suburbia, there in a layby. But the silence. Sound has always meant more to me than vision. Anyone can see anything. But it takes somebody special to hear, to really hear. I was special.

It was the silence of the desert, that's what changed me. Even me.

So thank you, dad, for stopping the car, and for turning off the engine. As so often with children, what you think is the main point is nothing. It's what just happens, unconsciously, that defines the decades.

Now I've got kids, and I wanted to show them the desert. We went last year, and they played in the burning sand, under a furnace sun, muffled in the enormous silence. Left alone, mostly. They say they still remember it, but maybe they don't. That's OK. Maybe they'll remember a feeling of light, or heat.

I'm lucky to know Feynan, and luckier to be able to return here with people I love. It's a long way, two hours' drive from anywhere, and then another half-an-hour off the road in a screeching wreck of a pickup that has Isaac's sister asking where the seatbelts are and why she isn't on her booster seat.

At the lodge Suleiman shakes our hand, we let the walls wrap us in the sound of hot stone, we climb the scorpion slopes across the stream-bed to fill our pockets with stripy sweetstones, Isaac calls them, then we walk out at sunset.

Every day they do this, the lodge guides, take who-

ever's staying and walk twenty minutes to a nearby ridge
to watch the sunset.

* * *

Coming here from outside, you'd think it was the
lodge—a beautifully evoked desert hotel, praised by
every starry-eyed travel writer lucky enough to make
it here—that has changed this place forever. Candle-lit,
solar-powered, environmentally conscious, set around
a shaded courtyard, with every room bedecked in Syrian silks and every meal healthy and organic, Feynan
Eco Lodge—or, rather, the skill of Nabil Tarazi, director
of the small company that runs it—has single-handedly
put Jordan on the global map of experiential wilderness
tourism.

But the lodge is only the latest catalyst, and it's been
here longer than you might imagine. It was designed
twenty-odd years ago by the rootsy Jordanian architect
Ammar Khammash to be a dig house for the archaeologists who spend months at a time in this ancient place.
The archaeologists have since moved elsewhere, but
that's why the bathrooms are so unexpectedly Spartan:
this is a luxury hotel retrofitted into a working building.

The archaeologists came here because of the mines.
Before tourism Feynan was known, if at all, for supplying
the Roman Empire with copper, then as now an essential
commodity. Its splintered hills hosted a vast, scorching
penal colony where Christians and other criminals broke
rocks, spirits and bones in what must have seemed a
limitless place of heat and terrible, memory-less death.

Hopeful dreamers wonder whether, in an earlier age,
these were also King Solomon's mines. And earlier still,

a hundred centuries earlier, Feynan—secreted in a topo-
graphical fold where the water of perpetually-flowing
streams pouring down from the mountain heights is
caught before draining away into the great alluvial fan
of the desert plains below—was one of the special places
where our hunter-gatherer ancestors put stones on top of
stones to make houses and chose to live together for the
very first time.

There are ghosts here. Feynan vibrates with them.

Now, it is semi-nomadic families who live here,
mostly from a tribe—the Azazmeh—that was split asun-
der by the Middle East wars of 1948. When a border was
drawn for the first time defining Israel, many Azazmeh
were trapped behind it. They suffered—and continue
to suffer—persecution under the Israelis, concentrated
onto tiny parcels of land around the city of Beer Sheba.
Many were expelled, including to Jordan. Their arrival
marked the start of our own generations of change in Feynan.

As the Rashaydeh tribe jockeyed to absorb the
Azazmeh newcomers in their midst, the Jordanian government arrived from the big city to quarry at Feynan,
seeking mineral wealth. Archaeologists took an interest
—wherever you go in the Middle East, you'll find that
British historians have been there before you—and then
so did Jordanian environmentalists, successfully halting
the quarrying and throwing an invisible border around
Feynan, calling it part of a protected nature reserve
linked to Dana, a hamlet looking down from the watered
mountain heights.

Nothing here is as it was. Many people still farm, but
fewer than before. Feynan is where wolves come out of
the corrugated canyons to steal people's sheep and goats.

It is where men stay up all night, patrolling in velvet solitude, to keep hyenas off the watermelon fields. I have sat
in Azazmeh tents in Feynan and had patriarchs describe
their journeys to Beer Sheba, telling me how much better
off their cousins are over there, how much richer. (And
I have also seen the Azazmeh around Beer Sheba, living
in grinding poverty under the stench of a chemical factory, their houses demolished, lacking electricity, water
or civil rights.)

So the lodge—which employs Azazmeh men as guides
and cooks, Azazmeh women as bakers and craftsworkers,
and Rashaydeh greybeards as drivers—has indeed transformed Feynan, but it is only the newest celebrant amid
three generations of continuous change here.

The place sings with newness. You feel the hundred
centuries as a hand in the small of your back, strong
enough to lean on, light enough to support your next
step. I don't know anywhere like it.

* * *

It's a twenty-minute walk from the lodge to the sunset point, on a stony path above a stony riverbed, beside stony hills. Suleiman, who is lithe and clear-eyed,
walking with the cat-like self-possession of the bedouin,
points out his family's tent—long and low, of black goat's
hair, in a hollow by the path—and I remember that I
drank coffee with his father the time before last, two or
three years ago, when his father told me he was worried
that none of his children would want to live in a tent
anymore.

We walk between the only buildings of significance
in Feynan, almost the only buildings of any kind: the

mosque and the school, opposite each other. One of the tangle-haired kids boots a hopelessly flat ball to Isaac. It's a characteristically disarming gesture of unexpected warmth and friendship in a strange place. Isaac's not much good at football but he responds, of course, and they share a kick-around.

The world's a playground.

* * *

Up on the ridge, Isaac, I didn't know.

While the others clustered together, I talked to Suleiman as he made a little fire between the rocks and set about brewing tea. Was that when you had the idea?

When you asked me how to make fire with sticks, I didn't know where your question came from. I told you a bit about rubbing between your palms, and how long and hard you have to rub to generate enough heat for a spark, and how you have to gather fluff and dry kindling first, and how I've never done it, but how you could use, yes, that stick looks about right.

I saw you go off and rub the stick on a rock between your palms, but then Suleiman pointed over to the place where you can see the sunset through the branches of an acacia tree, and I thought you might like that, so we went off that way. You were more interested in jumping from rock to rock and we all pretty much ignored the sunset, and when we came back Suleiman had finished making tea, and the fire was out, and it was only at that point, when you came to me distraught, with tears in your eyes, saying there was no fire but you wanted to make fire, that I properly understood.

The others were drinking their tea.

So Suleiman helped us bring a few rocks together to make a little hearth, and he gingerly flicked over one of the still-glowing sticks from the tea fire, and then we gathered tiny bits of kindling—which wasn't dry enough, really—and piled some on top of the fire-stick. Then he and you and your sister and me took turns.

Cheek to the dust.

Blow.

Face away to breathe.

Blow again.

It took a long time, because the kindling was bad. The call to prayer came and went, and we still blew. I wasn't sure it would catch, and neither was Suleiman.

But then it caught, and a flame appeared, and you loved it.

* * *

When I had the idea for us to come to Jordan, I thought we would do that walk to the ridge above Feynan so we could feel the glassy clink of the desert stones and think about a dry place. So we could see the sunset and think about light and dark. So we could hear the call to prayer —that haunting call to prayer, from the imam with the beautiful voice in that tiny mosque, the voice that brought someone to tears the last time I stood on that ridge and heard it—and I thought maybe I would try and tell you what the call to prayer is about.

I was prepared for all of those.

But instead you made fire up there, Isaac.

Fire.

It was the best thing ever. Better than all my plans.

And if you don't remember, that's OK too. We'll go

back to Feynan. Deserts matter, I reckon.

JORDAN: LISTENING TO THE LAND

Architecture / 2018 / AramcoWorld

Deep in the forests of oak and pine that cloak the hills of northern Jordan, down a side-road off a side-road, you'll find a long, low building of pale limestone. It represents the future for a new generation of environmental conservationists, and also embodies the design esthetic of a boundary-breaking Jordanian architect.

"Architecture is a sin," says Ammar Khammash, 57. "I don't want to be visible, and I don't want my buildings to be visible."

Standing in a building he designed, this unconventional man—artist, designer, engineer, geologist, musician and polymath—faces a view of dark-green treetops under spring sunshine. The forest is silent but for birdsong and cicadas. He names two world-famous 'starchitects'.

"I want to be the exact opposite of them," he says. "Architecture is not that important. Buildings should not become monuments, or luxury statements. They can be impressive without being expensive."

We are talking in the Royal Academy for Nature Conservation, designed by Khammash for Jordan's Royal Society for the Conservation of Nature (RSCN) and officially opened in 2015. It stands at the entrance to an RSCN-run nature reserve protecting forest land beside Ajloun, a town seventy kilometres north of the Jordanian capital Amman.

Though Khammash's small architectural practice can claim many prestigious private and governmental clients, he is best known for a string of RSCN commissions, ranging from a lodge in Dana, a remote mountain village in the south, to a restaurant and offices in the heart of Amman. His stripped-back designs using locally sourced materials, referencing vernacular traditions and exemplifying acute environmental sensitivity are on show in visitor reception centres, rangers' offices and rural guest houses all around Jordan, enhancing places that many tourists visit—and that many Jordanians cherish.

Chris Johnson, a British ecologist who worked with Khammash for twenty years, speaks of the architect's "uniquely Jordanian" style.

"Ammar has an amazing ability to create new buildings that are respectful of their surroundings and Jordan's cultural heritage," says Johnson, who directed conservation for the RSCN in the 1990s and from 2005 to 2013 led its sustainable tourism unit 'Wild Jordan'.

Growth in outreach has been mirrored by growth in skills development. Since 1997 the RSCN has trained around 250 specialists a year from Jordan and across the Middle East in management of protected areas, conservation research, ecotourism and socio-economic development. Around 2005 the idea emerged to formalise training in a single, dedicated building.

"We had been pioneering capacity-building in conservation throughout the region. With success came demand," says Johnson, who initiated and managed the project to build the new academy.

For RSCN director general Yehya Khaled, the academy pointed to a breakthrough in public education on the environment. "We wanted the academy to be a model, representing RSCN values [in] conservation and community development," he says.

A site was identified inside the Ajloun Forest Reserve but, as Khammash explains, "I kept passing a quarry just outside the reserve boundary—and I said 'Why should we cut another wound in nature, when we already have this cut? Let's fix this, and celebrate it as a human intervention.'"

He continues, with typical self-deprecation:

"Whoever was driving the last bulldozer in the last week this quarry was operating, back in the early '90s, never knew that he was designing the front elevation of my building for me. He left a cliff, and I followed it. This building is designed by chance."

Khammash had the quarry pit cleared but instead of bringing in stone for construction, he used the rubble, which would normally have been discarded. The result is external walls of unusually small limestone rocks, neatly fitted together. The impression is of a building at one with its setting, as if it has been lifted from the quarry complete and placed on the ridgetop.

To reach it from the road, Khammash designed what was (until he built a longer one last year) the longest masonry arch in Jordan, an elegant bridge extending for thirty metres over the now-empty quarry.

"This bridge has almost no foundation," he says. "Its lateral thrust is like when you take a cane and bend it across a corridor. It can't go anywhere, so the more load it takes the more it pushes into the quarry sides."

The bridge delivers you to the building's public entrance, a slot in one flank that opens to—almost nothing. The lobby, like its architect, impresses by stealth. You could cross this low, transitional room in four paces, but a glass wall in the opposite flank keeps the forest in view and the ambience is of spacious calm. Free of adornment, displaying a deliberately rough finish of raw concrete, it is artful.

Khammash calls it simply a "void" where the building's two functions meet: a restaurant in one wing generates income to help pay for the training courses that are run in the other wing. Turn right, and the restaurant area draws you out through airy interiors to shaded rear balconies woven about with foliage. But the heart of this building's beauty shows when you turn left.

Double-loaded corridors—ones that have doors opening on both sides—tend to be dark. Here, though, sunlight moves across the rubble-stone walls: Khammash has opened a glass roof above the corridor for illumination, and created an end-wall of windows facing west. In summer, cool winds flow through as natural ventilation.

The architect explains how he drew inspiration for this passageway—which is not straight, but sinuously angled—from Jordan's famous ancient city of Petra, where you enter through a towering cleft between mountains, lit from above by shafts of sunlight.

"The light pulls you in the right direction," he says. "And the bending is important. If you expose the whole length of the corridor, it's too much. Also, the bend mirrors the profile line of the quarry outside."

Underfoot, Khammash has used ceramic floor tiles that are familiar from Jordanian apartments—but with a twist.

"I specified the cheapest tile in Jordan," he says. "The poorest of the poor use it. But here we spread them wider and filled the gaps between each one. You end up with this interesting pattern, like a carpet with pulled threads."

This lack of pretension, eschewing the temptations of Italian marble, Scandinavian wood, or even plaster for the walls, can cause confusion: visitors seeing rough, concrete walls and cheap, gappy floor tiles ask when the building will be finished—and then tut when they hear it is.

"They think it's a joke, but we're demonstrating that cheap materials can be a good choice," says Khammash. "Materials pick up social value. People want to imitate Amman, using expensive imported stuff, but the result is a hotchpotch. This is a crude finish, but very durable, and should age nicely. It's a very rugged building."

Another consequence is a surprising minimalism. Khammash's balconies, for instance, narrow to the slenderest of cement edges, supported beneath by angled beams anchored in the smallest possible foundation. To stand on one is to fly above the trees.

But visuals tell only part of the story. The building, completed in 2013, deploys an array of environmentally progressive techniques from straw-based insulation and grey-water collection to geothermal energy for heating and cooling. During this two-year, $3.9-million construction project in dense woodland, not a single tree was felled.

Chris Johnson talks of Khammash's "artist's eye." For Khammash, synaesthesia underpins creativity.

"I'm into sound," he says. "Every time I see light on geological formations I hear music—it's like a waterfall hitting rocks, and the light is playing a sound. There's some strange connection in my brain. The sun plays this corridor differently according to the season and the time of day."

Once you tune into Khammash's aural architecture, you find it everywhere. It draws the sounds of the forest —creaking of trees, whistling of wind—into the building. And it sends the sounds of the building—voices, footsteps—spiralling together in unexpected pools and pockets.

"My dream is to teach a course of architecture for blind architects, to force architects only to use the ear, not the eye," he says. "Architecture has been hijacked by the visual. What about the sound of the building, the smell of the building, the idea of earthing, experiencing architecture through our feet?"

For the academy's conference hall, located within its western cantilever, the architect examined how opera houses manage acoustics with walls of slatted wood, which dampen reverberation. Adapting the science to the local context, he built walls of cinder blocks—but then laid them sideways, so that their slatted, open cores face into the room.

"This is a nice, interesting way of using these blocks. Sound stays in the holes. You don't need a microphone for a speaker to be heard clearly at the back of the hall," he says.

Khammash's architecture blends here with conceptual art.

"People could write notes and push them into the holes, or keep pencils in there. Another idea was to bring local students to fill the upper third of the walls with branches and twigs pushed into these blocks. Wood is good for acoustics, and this could also help people feel they own the building—they could come back and say, 'You see that branch? I put it there ten years ago.'"

Khammash warms to his theme.

"Architecture is a beginning. Let others add to your work. You see this in art installations, but architecture can do it too. Buildings can change, if you just give people the skeleton to start with."

In 2016 this unique building was shortlisted for the Aga Khan Award for Architecture—"a great privilege," says Yehya Khaled, not least for international recognition of the building's potential to deliver a new generation of conservationists. He tells me the RSCN is developing curricula for training programmes to run here with international partners including the University of Montana, and that it has brought local socio-economic projects developing biscuit-making and handmade soap production into the building. Rebranding the academy as 'Wild Jordan Ajloun' is next, which will help consolidate efforts to deploy this remarkable asset for tourism as well as education.

Khammash watches with pride.

"Architecture is problem-solving," he says. "This is the spark for me, and every time I design, that's in my subconscious. Can we solve the problem without the building? If I can, I will. The site is the architect, and I listen to it. Ultimately I'm just a draughtsman, a technician under the site's command."

JORDAN: SUFFERING WITH LIBYANS

Politics & society / 2012 / BBC

For hoteliers in the Jordanian capital Amman, January can be miserable. It's the lowest of low seasons for Western tourists, who prefer the temperate months of spring and autumn, and long-stay Arab tourists, who escape the heat of the Gulf to spend cooler summer holidays near the Med, won't arrive for another six months.

Yet this week [January 2012], even in the depths of winter, the smiles are broad all across Jordan's hospitality sector, thanks to an unexpected Libyan windfall.

Amman is a highland city. When I drove in from the airport it was not so much raining as condensing: the misty air was grey and saturated, and it was bitter cold, high above sea level amid precipitous urban hills.

The lobby of my hotel was steamy and crowded with

pretty scruffy-looking characters, lounging in tracksuits on the sleek, ultra-modern furniture, arguing in an accented Arabic I couldn't place.

"We are suffering a bit," hotel manager Ibrahim Karajeh told me. "These Libyans are not well educated and they talk loudly, but they're making good revenue. This is very low season for us but I'm having to turn business away."

Jordan was a key Arab ally for Libya's rebel armies during last year's revolution, supplying logistical and military aid. Now, it seems, payback time has come. Lacking both hospital infrastructure and medical expertise, post-war Libya is flying thousands of its citizens abroad for treatment, including at Jordanian hospitals, widely regarded as the best in the Middle East. Medical bills, lodging and three meals a day are being paid for by Libya's new government, the National Transitional Council. Officials tour Amman weekly, settling hotel and hospital bills in cash—and handing out 300 US dollars per person per week as pocket money.

The arrangement began last summer, for fighters who had been seriously injured in combat—but the trickle has become a flood since the death of Colonel Gaddafi three months ago.

I sat in on a discussion between Michel Nazzal, president of the Jordan Hotel Association, and Nayef al-Fayez, Jordan's Minister of Tourism. Every three-, four- and five-star hotel in the capital is full. Twenty-six planes arrived last week from Libya. Amman, they told me, is hosting 14,000 Libyans.

But the minister is not complaining. "We need them!" he said, with a genial smile. "It's good for business."

That's undeniable. I would estimate Libya is pumping

around fifteen million dollars a week into Jordan's re-tail economy. That excludes income from hospital bills, which could also be substantial.

In a modest, resource-poor country which saw a forty percent drop in tourism last year, that's no small wind-fall. According to hotelier Charl Twal, the Libyans are "saving Amman".

Across town in the private, three-hundred-bed Jor-dan Hospital, administrator Amany Khatab told me that since November they'd treated 465 Libyans as inpatients —but many more as outpatients. "Minor cases would have surgery during the day," she explained, "then go back to the hotel, and return next morning."

She walked me along broad, brightly lit corridors, spotless and quiet. Doctors smiled in greeting.

At bed 128 on the first floor, 62-year-old Saleh Muham-mad Suleiman passed a tired hand over a white beard. He'd arrived three weeks earlier from his home in the eastern Libyan city of Tobruk for treatment for chronic hypertension. "We were relying on foreign doctors," he told me. "But they all went home during the war."

Two of Suleiman's sons fought against Gaddafi. "Libya has a good future," he said, gesturing with his cannulated right hand. "The people running the government are young. They know what is best."

On another corridor, Ali Muhammad Albusaifi was on crutches. His leg had been fractured in Zawiya, early in the fighting. Then he'd fought in Zintan, before spending the summer smuggling weapons into government-held Tripoli. "We'd come in at night," the 24-year-old told me, "bringing guns in rubbish bins or under cars."

Then, in October, in Bani Walid, his convoy had taken a direct hit. He'd been thrown high in the air, landing on rocks, breaking his nose and teeth, damaging his hearing and tearing muscles in both legs.

"It's a fantastic feeling," he said, with a hollow-eyed smile. "But we never imagined any of this before."

What had life been like under Gaddafi, I asked.

"I don't want to rewind," he said, gazing at the floor. "We have strong national bonds—" and he twined his fingers together to demonstrate. Then he shrugged angrily, a mixed-up young man, who'd already seen too much violence in his life.

With pathos, and some despair, he added, "I want to keep on fighting. I just don't know who."

Even though Libya is successfully outsourcing treatment, healing, it seems, must start at home.

BAHRAIN: THE BURNT PLACE

Culture / 2008 / Gulf Life

"**F**ollow me."

Ezmiralda Kabbani pushed her oversized sunglasses up onto her forehead and squeezed through a narrow doorway. From outside on the hot, dusty lane it looked like nothing, just an anonymous door in an anonymous alley.

I followed her inside—and we stood, suddenly, in air-conditioned comfort, on a polished wood floor. The outside glare was replaced by tinted daylight flooding a broad, circular space through a huge skylight supported on pointed arches. Shelves of books in English and Arabic lined the wall to my left; half a dozen computer screens stood ranged to one side. The interior felt calm and architecturally deft, using areas of natural and artificial light to create airy, open spaces within what was only a small, narrow building.

"This is the children's library," Ezmiralda said. "It's

called 'Iqra', meaning "read". It's only for the local children of Muharraq, somewhere they can come and take some time, play, daydream, read a book." She looked at her watch. "And it's almost storytime."

As if on cue, twenty or so kids clattered in through the door and flung themselves down onto floor cushions under that great skylight. Local teacher and part-time storyteller Dana Abul followed them in, perched herself in an alcove, settled her audience, chose a storybook and began to read aloud, acting out all the parts herself.

It was great to watch, and chatting with Dana and the kids gave a glimpse into the ordinary life of Muharraq—a part of Bahrain most visitors don't even know exists.

Muharraq island lies just northeast of Bahrain's capital Manama, connected to it by several highway-carrying causeways. A tiny dot of land, just seventeen square kilometres in area, it has long held an importance far beyond its size. From 300 BCE, when the Greeks held sway, the island was known as Arados, distinct from its larger neighbour, Bahrain island (known as Tylos). Historians theorise that the name *muharraq*—which means "the burnt place"—might commemorate some great fire here in antiquity. By the nineteenth century, Muharraq was Bahrain's capital, the centre of government and hub of the region's pearl industry.

I wandered through whitewashed alleyways to the building which best evokes that period of Muharraq's history, the Shaikh Isa House. Begun around 1800, this palace served as the residence of Shaikh Isa bin Ali al-Khalifa, ruler of Bahrain from 1869 to 1932. Showing only blank walls to the street—it occupies an entire city block—inside, it displays ornately carved arabesque designs around every doorway, niche and pointed arch. Its mud-brick walls are faced with gypsum, which glitters white in the glare of the sun but has an almost alabaster-like luminescence in the darker, cooler interior.

Each of the house's four austere courtyards is linked to the next by a labyrinth of narrow passageways. Massively thick walls, up to a metre wide, and small, deep-set windows help keep the sun's heat at bay, as does the building's distinctive windtower. This classic feature of Gulf architecture was a precursor to air-conditioning —a square, open tower built high above roof level to catch any passing breezes and direct them down into the rooms.

I met up with Ezmiralda again to see another of Muharraq's renovation projects, the Shaikh Ebrahim Centre for Culture and Research. She explained that Shaikh Ebrahim bin Mohammed al-Khalifa was a late nineteenth-century Bahraini writer who led a cultural salon from his Muharraq home, where intellectuals would gather to debate issues of the day. Today, a contemporary equivalent has arisen under Shaikha Mai bint Mohammed al-Khalifa, a member of the ruling family and a strong advocate for Bahrain's cultural heritage. She has led efforts to restore Shaikh Ebrahim's home to serve as a national cultural centre, hosting academics, poets, musicians, writers and critics in a year-round programme of lectures, debates and performances.

By drawing donations and corporate sponsorship, the Shaikh Ebrahim Centre—now holding an intimate, galleried auditorium seating around 150—has restored several traditional buildings around Muharraq and Manama. The Iqra children's library was one. A short walk through the lanes stood another, the stunning Abdullah al-Zayed House, where exquisite *mashrabiya* pierced wooden panelling and delicately carved gypsum are heightened by fanlight panels above each door, fitted with colourful stained glass in red, green, blue and yellow—another traditional method, I was told, of reducing the sun's glare indoors. Al-Zayed was founder of the country's first newspaper, *Bahrain*, in 1939, and his restored house, set around a covered courtyard, now serves as the Press Heritage Centre, housing newspaper archives and a historical research library.

Then there's the Korar House, where a group of women were working with complex webs of golden thread and natural fibres to produce traditional embroidery, and the Mohammed bin Faris House, former home of a pioneer Bahraini artist and now an arts centre showcasing performances of traditional music.

It was a real eye-opener, this series of beautifully restored buildings, hidden away in palm-shaded lanes I wouldn't have thought to explore. Yet the district was no museum piece. As I wandered out onto the main streets, Muharraq's shopkeepers were busy and traffic was flowing. A regrettably brief hour or two in the old souk hinted at depths of cultural heritage in Muharraq— oral, intangible—that grand restoration projects cannot reach. I wanted to linger.

QATAR: HISTORY ON THE SCREEN

Digitisation / 2016 / unpublished

They could so easily be cynical. Facing each other across a horseshoe of tables, girls on one side, boys on the other, these teenagers might, in other situations, preen, pose, scoff.

Instead, there's an air of concentration. Heads crowd together. Shoulders hunch as fingers swipe to and fro across tablet screens, or tap at laptop keyboards.

"I like it a lot—it's like I'm looking at history on the screen," comments Abdelrahman, a college freshman majoring in mass communications.

Hebzi, studying public policy, has been absorbed in scrolling chunks of text in Arabic and English. "The translation is very good. I'm very impressed."

High-school student Ameera gestures at her tablet in wonder. "You're holding a map from 1880 on your 21st-century iPad," she says.

Corralled in a room at the Hamad Bin Khalifa University student centre, in Qatar's capital city, Doha, these eight students formed one of the first groups to test a new web portal dubbed the Qatar Digital Library (QDL). This online resource—part of the Qatar National Library's collections—is the result of an ongoing ten-year project to digitise and publish millions of documents relating to the history of the Gulf.

The project, developed in partnership with the British Library, is an endeavour worth investigating on its own merits.

But this is a tale less about libraries, and more about how nations grow intellectual underpinnings. As Qatar and other Gulf countries redefine their relationships to the former colonial power, Britain, they are also reclaiming their own history. That's happening metaphorically, with local perspectives emerging amid critical analysis of accepted narratives, but also literally, through projects like the QDL.

Most historical source material on the Middle East is held in archives in far-away capitals: London's British Library is just one example. Until now, only scholars resident nearby, or with the resources to travel and request access in person, have been able to study it.

It is those scholars, therefore, who have written the history.

But the QDL—the most ambitious of the region's digitisation programmes—is now giving anyone with an internet connection, wherever they might be, free access to the historical sources.

This universality is unprecedented. The sources are being returned—virtually—to their countries of origin through digitisation, and opened to all. Previously accepted histories, ideas and even identities can be tested anew by an incomparably wider readership than before.

In short, the QDL heralds a realignment of who writes the Middle East's history.

* * *

The QDL project developed from discussions held in 2010 between the British Library and the Qatar Foundation for Education, Science and Community Development, a nonprofit organisation set up by the Qatari royal family whose aim is to shift Qatar to a knowledge-based economy.

First, why Britain?

The Gulf was never formally part of the British Empire, but came under colonial administration after being targeted for its trade potential in the seventeenth century by Britain's East India Company. In 1858, the East India Company became an executive arm of the British government, known as the India Office.

The India Office administered a swathe of territory stretching from modern-day Burma as far west as Aden in Yemen, including a string of settlements along both shores of the Gulf. As technology improved during the nineteenth century, British administrators began to realise the importance of the Gulf as a conduit, particularly for seaborne trade with India. Telegraph cables laid along the Gulf's seabed established direct lines of communication between London and Bombay.

The records those administrators kept, over more than three hundred years—government papers, diplomatic dispatches, letters, diaries, financial receipts, maps, sketches, photographs, notes and more—were eventually transferred to London after the abolition of the India Office in 1947.

There they remain, millions of documents occupying nine miles of shelving within the British Library—the most important collection of primary source material on Gulf history in the world.

"All libraries are changing how they serve their patrons. They now need to provide access both to physical materials and to online content," says John Van Oudenaren, a programme director on international outreach at the Library of Congress in Washington, DC. "It has always been a mission of libraries to provide copies of documents in their holdings to interested researchers [and] readers. This previously was done by photocopying and microfilming. In the nineteenth century the United States even employed clerks who would go to libraries in Europe and copy by hand documents relating to US history. Now this is being done digitally."

In the 1990s, archives around the world launched large-scale digitisation projects, including national libraries in Norway, South Korea, Germany and the United States. The trend was also felt in the Arab World: Saudi Arabia began digitising its national archives, and cooperation with European institutions enabled smaller collections in the region to digitise, including the al-Aqsa Mosque Library in Jerusalem, and the Fouad Debbas collection of historic photographs in Beirut.

By the late 2000s, with the rise in global influence of Gulf states including the UAE and Qatar, the pace of cultural cooperation began to accelerate. Richard Gibby, of the British Library, takes up the story.

"The British Library's mission [includes] making our collections available worldwide, so we were looking for partners, particularly in the Gulf region in respect of the India Office Records. At the same time, the Qatar Foundation was interested in advancing education and community development in Qatar and the Gulf. There was a coming together."

* * *

After more than two years of discussions, in 2012 the British Library and the Qatar Foundation signed a partnership agreement, launching a mammoth ten-year digitisation project. This, unusually, included complete publication online as well as a programme of contextual pieces to help guide readers around the mass of material, written by the British Library's specialists.

More than forty full-time staff were taken on, integrated alongside the British Library's existing expertise on curation, technology, and procurement. An entire floor of the British Library building in London was taken over and remodelled to accommodate them.

With the quantity of material involved, project managers devised a new workflow. First, batches of records are identified for retrieval from the British Library's storage shelves. Phase one of the digitisation project, from 2012 to 2014, focused on two such collections—from Bushire (now Bushehr in Iran), on the Gulf's northern shore, which was Britain's main base in the region between 1763 and 1946; and from Bahrain, opposite on the southern shore, a port since the Bronze Age and long an economic hub for its pearl fisheries. British officials stationed in both towns generated vast amounts of paperwork over the centuries, filed—sometimes carelessly—in thousands of boxes, bound books or loose-leaf files.

Conservators receiving those files work first to preserve each paper item contained within. Specialist researchers then re-catalogue each item, which may have spent decades unnoticed, sometimes because of poor labelling. They add identifying keywords and subject tags —known as "metadata"—to the new digital catalogue record.

The item is then carried a few metres across the office to imaging technicians, who scan everything to do with it, including covers, ribbon ties, folds, marks, seals, stamps, additional notes, even damage. They may also photograph it, to preserve as much detail of the archival original as possible.

Computer specialists then run Optical Character Recognition (OCR) software on the scanned file to convert typescripts—and even some manuscripts—into searchable text. This OCR process is relatively straightforward for English type, with its separate letters, but notoriously difficult in Arabic, whose printed text uses variable, cursive letter forms. Experience gathered over the last few years on this project, Richard Gibby explains, has helped refine and advance Arabic OCR software worldwide.

Then, the scan is uploaded to the digital library itself and published online, where it can be viewed at the QDL's website www.qdl.qa. Access to the site is free, without registration, and all content is navigable in English and Arabic.

Digitisation thus creates a preservation copy, a surrogate that allows conservators to better safeguard the original. It also represents the chance to create new catalogue records with detailed metadata for intuitive search, and to introduce the document to new readerships. Fresh curatorial connections between archive institutions often follow.

Academics, too, see tangible benefits.

"The QDL has afforded a crucial resource for students who seek to conduct archival research for which little to no funds are available for travel to London," says Rosie Bsheer, professor of history at Yale University. "I have had two or three students each semester who base their research papers on these archives."

Bsheer continues: "[The QDL] will not only break the financial, physical and other barriers of conducting research on the Gulf and its peoples, which have been marginalised from history. But, in reading these digital archives against the grain, it will also allow us to study the politics of knowledge production more broadly."

Digitisation, however, does have drawbacks. For many researchers, the most important discoveries are often the unexpected ones—a misfiled document unearthed while leafing through unrelated material, or getting your hands on the file you thought you wanted, only to spot something even more interesting just along the same shelf. Even with meticulous metadata, such serendipity largely evaporates online.

* * *

Phase one of the British Library Qatar Foundation partnership ended in October 2014, when the QDL website was launched to the public with around 150,000 pages online. By late 2016, well into phase two (which runs until December 2018), the QDL held almost a million pages, and the digitisation process had been expanded to include records spanning the years between 1600 and 1967, adding material from the British administrative posts at Kuwait and Muscat, and also including tens of thousands of documents from the British Library's holdings of Arabic manuscripts on science, medicine, astronomy, mathematics, and geography dating back to the ninth century.

"This is unique in its scale and scope," says Richard Gibby. "The British Library has many other partnerships, but what makes this project special is the variety of content we are covering—and the amount of metadata we are creating for search."

"The QDL is a magnificent resource for finding out what life here was like, what foreign perceptions were like, who the people were, the geography as well as the history," says Dr Frederick Nesta, senior lecturer in library and information studies at University College London's teaching facility in Doha. "The standards are very good. It was very hard for me and my students to find things that were wrong."

Yet the QDL was conceived as part of an even larger project, to create a national library almost from scratch. In 2012, at the fiftieth anniversary celebrations for Doha's Dar al-Kutub (an Arabic term usually translated as "national library"), Sheikha Moza bint Nasser, chair of the Qatar Foundation, announced the establishment of a new library that would replace and extend Dar al-Kutub. The new Qatar National Library (QNL) would have a three-fold function, she said, serving as a national archive, a specialist academic research library and a metropolitan city library open to the public.

"Most national libraries sit on the hill and collect things, but [the QNL] is similar in concept to the National Library of Singapore, in terms of outreach and development—a research library, a public library and a children's library," says Frederick Nesta, who runs a one-year programme to train local librarians for the QNL.

Dutch architect Rem Koolhaas was commissioned to design the QNL building. While construction work continued, the library began operating digitally from temporary premises, opening online access to its own catalogues as well as global library databases, devising public education programmes targeting children, students and researchers, and launching the QDL as part of its digital collections.

However, despite the branding, relatively little of the QDL's content is about Qatar as a nation. It's much broader than that, encompassing the Gulf as a whole—and beyond. So why is Qatar doing this?

"There is not much written history about Qatar," says Claudia Lux, project director of the QNL (which awaits a physical home in Koolhaas's new building). "But people from Qatar are not just from Qatar. From Kuwait to Saudi Arabia to Bahrain, the Gulf region is of interest to them. Most of the Gulf countries have copied historical material about their country, but they keep it in research institutes. I don't believe it's a good thing to have all these copies in different institutes. The QDL is really something we want to showcase as an example. Hopefully others will follow and open up their material."

There is also the issue of soft power—the ability of a country to project its values and improve its international standing without the use of force. Acutely conscious of global attention in the build-up to its hosting of the football World Cup in 2022, Qatar is using its self-declared role as a pioneer of intellectual society-building as a soft power lever.

Yet deeper motivations are also in play.

"My sense is that it's something that started with

Hamad bin Khalifa [Qatar's emir 1995-2013] and Sheikha Moza [Hamad's wife]," says Gerd Nonneman, professor of international relations and dean of the School of Foreign Service at Georgetown University's campus in Doha, who has studied Qatar for three decades. "It's a reimagining of what Qatar could be—and part of it, I've become convinced over the years, is a genuine commitment to kick-starting a flowering of education culture, scientific development, human capacity-building. [The QDL] is one component of that. The fact that it might also have other rationales, about branding, about prestige, about visibility, doesn't mean that it's not also genuine in substance."

For Nonneman, investment in mass digitisation—and, crucially, publication—of historical sources points to a top-level desire to reshape society.

"A national museum very often is not about simply giving unbiased access to historical documentation—it's part of a nation-building exercise, creating a national image. But working with an external collection to make existing documentation available for anybody—that's different. It's part of nation-building, but at one remove. It's saying, 'We are the kind of nation that opens this [material] up to people.'"

"The QDL may help change perceptions about access to knowledge," continues Nonneman. "The very idea that something one sees doesn't necessarily have to be 'right' to be acceptable, but is a piece of evidence that people ought to be able to judge for themselves—that's crucial in building critical thinking skills."

He suggests there is extra value to the idea of creating a digital library such as the QDL.

"There are lots of ways in which people can be helped to engage with knowledge and information. How do you draw in kids? Young people? It's not just about books. [The QDL] is potentially a very exciting way of getting students into the whole idea of examining evidence. With there being relatively little hard evidence of the past here—a lot of it was lived experience—there's a real thirst for engaging with what things were like. And there it is, right in front of them on their computers, to which they always have access. That's an exciting tool."

Yet principles of free academic inquiry contrast with Freedom House's assessment of Qatar as "not free". Amnesty International called Qatar's 2014 cybercrimes law "a major setback for freedom of expression", and Qatari writer Mohammed Al-Ajami was only released from prison in March [2016], having served five years of a fifteen-year sentence for writing a poem deemed insulting to the monarch.

The British Library and Qatar National Library both hold copies of the digitised archive but Richard Gibby's expectation is that the portal—currently hosted by Amazon—will eventually be transferred for hosting in Qatar.

That could expose material to manipulation by Qatari government censors.

"That was discussed very clearly right from the beginning," says Gibby. "Both sides made very clear to each other that there is no suggestion this will be censored. To date that has been borne out. We, the British Library, are trusting [the Qatar Foundation] and our faith is in them."

"Digitisation also allows for increased control of archival documents, as well as [closer] monitoring of what records any given researcher is trying to access," says Rosie Bsheer, who offers a clear take on the merit of the QDL project. "Despite Qatar's egregious record on civil liberties, which is in large part sustained by the support of world powers, we should welcome any endeavour to make archives more accessible, while critiquing the ways in which knowledge is organised and categorised."

* * *

The QDL's potential resonates with the Doha students given the chance to test it out.

"The new generation are going to use technology even more than us," says Ameera, 17. "We're not connected enough to our history—it's nice to give [that connection] in a new way."

"An online library is more beneficial in today's world than having the physical paper," adds Nasser Marzouq, 19, a college freshman. "It's better to have an electronic copy that everyone can write notes on than to have to go all the way to the library to see the [original]. We don't have a lot of recorded history from our perspective, so when you see a document online, that makes a difference. It's not a person behind the screen who typed it up, it's the actual signed letter from a hundred years ago in front of me."

That thirst for knowledge of past lives extends beyond the doings of colonial administrators. Qatar is currently hosting multiple projects, in both public and private spheres, devoted to oral history and what the United Nations Educational, Scientific, and Cultural Organisation (UNESCO) has termed "intangible cultural heritage"— meaning all those elements of culture that can't be placed in display cabinets, such as stories, poems, songs, recipes and ideas.

"There's a danger of Qatar losing its history, as the

country modernises," says Nasser al-Khori, of Qatar
Foundation. "[We want] to modernise while keeping hold
of culture. A lot of our history is shared through storytelling and we don't have written archives like the British Library—it's very interesting to see the perspectives
in the QDL's material. And these resources are online. We
can show [QDL scans] to our grandparents, and they can
tell us if they believe something [different] happened."

Digitisation has global ramifications. During the late
2000s, teams at the Library of Congress, the Bibliotheca
Alexandrina in Egypt and UNESCO developed the World
Digital Library (WDL), conceived as a platform for sharing of cultural works and archival resources on the open
web. The WDL launched in 2009 with more than thirty
partner institutions around the world, including Qatar.

John Van Oudenaren at the Library of Congress—who
has directed the WDL since its inception—told me how
the QNL contributes rare books, manuscripts and maps
to the WDL, and coordinates collaboration across the
Middle East.

"The WDL has partners in Egypt, Iraq, Oman, Qatar,
Saudi Arabia and other Arab countries. Our goal is to
have at least one partner in every country in the world,
as well as to increase the number and variety of Arabic-
language content on the WDL," he said.

The WDL—and a similar European Union project
named Europeana—neither own nor digitise their own
material. Instead, they act as aggregators, presenting
metadata on works held by (and digitised by) their partner institutions under a single digital roof. But they can
only exist if the institutions that hold primary source
material are able to digitise their holdings in the first
place—which is why Qatar's initiative to digitise the

British Library's records on the Gulf has such profound implications.

Sipping coffee in Doha, student Nasser Marzouq grasps the potential.

"Maybe we'll reverse it, and one day have our own archives about the British," he says, perhaps only half-joking.

QATAR: NOTHING BUT STORIES

Culture / 2014 / High Life

Some names have been changed.

In the Place of Snakes, on the grassless plains west of the Qatari capital, Doha, businessman Hasan al-Khalifa tucks his feet underneath him and directs his eldest son, Abdullah, out to the paddocks behind the house.

"Before, we had nothing. Only talking," Hasan says to me, eyes twinkling above a pepper-and-salt beard.

"Home and family counted as school, and stories were part of the job of parenting. Women would tell stories about the home, relationships. Men would tell stories about the world outside. But now, things are moving too fast."

He looks out to the palm groves at the edge of the courtyard. Shadows move imperceptibly across hot stone.

Then Abdullah returns, bringing a tin bowl brimming

with white froth. From similarly open-hearted encounters across Arabia I know the taste of camel's milk, fresh from the udder. Warm, sweet and refreshing, it is deliciously clean on the tongue. The mark of a man here is how he treats his guests. Hasan leans over and encourages me to take a date.

In other countries, food is a motivation for interaction. In the Arab world, hospitality is the motivation, and food simply the expression.

But Qatar is an unusual place to be drinking camel's milk. As commonly perceived, this astonishingly wealthy nation—like its Gulf neighbours Dubai, Abu Dhabi and the rest—is spending its billions building museums and galleries in an effort to buy a place in world culture, having no culture of its own.

Qatar was never a centre of urban civilisation, it's true. It also lacks a tradition of artistic sophistication. But don't be too quick to judge. Not all civilisation is urban.

Qatar feels like a work in progress, whose most interesting aspects are only now, slowly, being revealed. How does a small country in the midst of social change that has catapulted it from desperate poverty to, literally, the richest nation in the world in the space of two generations keep hold of its roots? Wealth and a reliance on imported labour have changed Qatari society forever, but has everything familiar been jettisoned? How can Qatar remember where it came from?

"The best people for that are the older generation," says Mohammed Abu Hindi, of the Qatar National Museum (QNM). Abu Hindi heads the rather grey-sounding Research and Collection Department. But in truth, his work at the QNM—which is due to open late next year—breaks new ground.

The buzzword is 'intangible cultural heritage'. Adopted by UNESCO in 2008 to sit alongside the already recognised concept of World Heritage Sites, 'intangible cultural heritage' refers to all those elements of culture that don't fit into display cabinets: stories, poems, songs, recipes, ideas and so on. With only a few objects to display, culled from the handful of archaeological digs undertaken in this tiny country, and no literary tradition to draw on, the QNM is all about intangible cultural heritage.

Rather than collecting artefacts, Qatar is collecting stories.

In the National Museum's case, this takes the form of oral histories. Over the last three years, researchers have gone out into the back streets and the villages to talk to those who remember the way things used to be. They've so far gathered around a hundred and fifty interviews with men and women, Qataris and foreigners, some on video, some audio, and a few—since, for reasons of cultural modesty, some Qatari women refuse to allow their voice to be recorded—only in transcription.

These memories tell of the hardships of life before oil wealth, and what happened when the big multinationals first arrived.

One of those who remembers is Khalifa al-Sayed.

"In the 1960s Doha was a cluster of villages," he tells me. "You'd bring your donkey to the souk, to pick up sugar, salt, kerosene. It would be rice for breakfast, lunch and dinner. I worked for Shell at that time, fifteen days straight on an oil rig. Every night there was nothing to do except tell tales."

For al-Sayed, those evenings were a chance to hone storytelling skills picked up as a youngster.

"At home my grandfather would build a fire, make milky ginger tea and then tell stories," he recalls. "When it came to my turn, I would tell them better!"

Now a journalist and playwright, al-Sayed has built his career on stories, some straight retellings of the past —the oral history being catalogued by the National Museum—but many drawn from the rich wellspring of folkloric tales that underlies Arab culture. He regularly goes into schools, encouraging the next generation in the same way he was encouraged himself.

Sipping sweet coffee, al-Sayed paints a word-picture of the days before oil, when the Gulf relied on pearls. Ships from Kuwait, Bahrain and Dubai, often with crew drawn from as far afield as Iraq and India, would gather at Qatar's pearling grounds. During the day divers would hunt for oysters. By night, songs and stories would go round, telling legends of sea-monsters, stars battling in the sky, sailors transformed into fish and human destiny guided by the appearance of a *jinni* (genie—a fiery spirit) or a *ghul* (ghoul—a shapeshifting demon). Stories would change with each retelling, mixing cultures and traditions.

Outsiders know the 1001 Nights—Aladdin, Sinbad and all—but just as potent were local stories that would circulate in every family, grandparents yarning to grandchildren about the exploits of tribal ancestors.

"These stories open up a different world," says journalism graduate Mariam Dahrouj, who spent 2010 travelling the country with two friends, Shatha Farajallah and Sara al-Khalfan, to document stories of Qatari life before oil. They published voice recordings and transcriptions on a website they called Swalif, a dialect word meaning chitchat. The site has lapsed, but plans are afoot to resurrect it, and possibly to incorporate their work into the QNM's archive.

"Stories were the only way to preserve our culture," says Umm Khalaf, another of Qatar's traditional story-tellers. "My mum would tell stories all day, round the house."

Now in her sixties, Umm Khalaf has become something of a local celebrity, retelling traditional stories to new audiences at festivals and even on TV. Many rely on archetypes shared in the European tradition—wicked stepmothers, Cinderella-like girls outwitting older sisters, odd little Rumpelstiltskin characters, and so on.

I ask Umm Khalaf for her favourite. On cushions in a traditional goat-hair tent, dressed in orange silks, her face concealed (from me, a man) behind a *batoola* face-mask, she grins and embarks on a complicated telling of the legend of Bu Darya (meaning "Old Man of the Sea" in Farsi), a water-genie who would kidnap unwary pearl divers and sink ships.

I don't catch it all, but the wide gaps in my understanding of Qatari dialect are filled by Sheikha Nora al-Thani, alongside me. Aunt to Qatar's ruling emir, Sheikha Nora directs the Qatar Heritage and Identity Centre (QHIC). While the National Museum devotes itself to oral history, the QHIC's mission is to collect folktales.

"Stories represent our cultural identity," says Qatar University sociology professor Dr Kaltham al-Ghanim, who has been collecting stories for twenty-five years. "Hollywood has crashed into our lives, and people watch movies now instead of listening to stories—but it's very important for the next generation to be more confident about what they have."

That lesson is being taken to heart: filmmakers across

the Arab world are starting to find a voice. In 2012 a team of animators in Doha under director Rahab Elewaly produced *Rain*. This twelve-minute short, made in a distinctive silhouette style reminiscent of twentieth-century animator Lotte Reiniger, was based on one of Khalifa al-Sayed's folktales about how a traveller stranded in the desert finds hospitality.

Over coffee in the heart of Doha's Souk Waqif, Elewaly explains how she was able to draw in British musician Nitin Sawhney to write the film's compelling soundtrack.

"There's just something about telling a story that lets everyone's imagination run wild," she laughs.

The fine line where oral history shades into storytelling is also where Mohanalakshmi Rajakumar works. She completes the triangle of Qatar's ongoing quest for stories by helping to foster the development of creative writing. A professor of English, her *Qatari Voices* anthology of stories by twenty-one local writers represents pushback against conservative resistance to the unfamiliar freedoms of fiction-writing. Her own novels have followed, as has Sophia al-Maria's *The Girl Who Fell To Earth* (2012), which Rajakumar characterises as "the first Qatari memoir—a really important book."

"Writing is becoming a way of remembering," Rajakumar says. "Where people are reticent, fiction becomes another way to tell a truth."

Back in the Place of Snakes, Hasan al-Khalifa stokes up the fire while we sip bitter cardamom coffee and chat about his father's poetry.

As the sunset fades, a breeze brings the sound of chirping from the palms.

"We have nothing but stories," says Hasan.

And I think—that's really all that any of us have.

UAE: VILLAGES AND OASES

Travel / 2009 / The Independent

"Dubai?" The camel farmer plumped his cushions, shifted onto the other buttock and took another sip of coffee. "Dubai is not Arab. There's nothing there."

He paused, and a cool breath of evening wind brought us a whiff of the desert—dry, subtle and serious, reminding me of a foxed paperback. We sat with our backs to the Empty Quarter, picking at the remains of dinner as the twilight gathered.

"The only place where you can find Arab culture now," he continued, "is in the small villages and the oases."

As the stars came out, I thanked them. Most tourists, when they visit the United Arab Emirates, never get to meet a single Emirati, whisked from hotel to mall in an air-conditioned bubble of expat culture. Four-fifths of the population—and almost everybody involved in tourism—is not Emirati.

But, as ever, there's no need to take what you're given. I set out to avoid all the urban flummery of the tallest this and most expensive that. It's not as if there's a lack of hinterland to explore. Abu Dhabi emirate, the largest of the UAE's seven regions, is about the size of the Irish Republic.

The first imperative was to get out of the city. I headed east to al-Ain, an oasis on the border with Oman that has been settled for millennia, since long before the coastal cities were even thought of. Sheikh Zayed, founder of the UAE, and Sheikh Khalifa, the current president, were born here.

Yet far from being hidebound, al-Ain is like a breath of fresh air after the sweaty commercialism of the coast. Though it's hot, it's the comfortable dry heat of the desert, and there's none of Dubai's Napoleon complex on show. The low-rise streets are shaded by palms and *ghaf* trees, fragrant with jasmine in the evenings. I strolled past ordinary clothes shops, emporia selling cheap radios and the Bin Khumairy Smoking Goods Company, where Mohamed from Shiraz talked me through thirteen different mixes of water-pipe tobacco.

Most people are still from somewhere else—you see more *shalwar kameez* than *kandoura*—yet al-Ain has a higher proportion of Emirati nationals than any other city in the country. I asked around for somewhere good to eat, and several people directed me to the Falcon, a shabby-looking curry house behind Pizza Hut. True to the hype it served exquisite rogan josh for about £1, yet almost all my fellow diners were Arab—normal for al-Ain, extremely unusual for the Gulf.

The oasis for which al-Ain ("The Spring") is named fills a part of the city centre with palm groves and lush gardens irrigated by ancient *falaj* channels. I walked one afternoon on cool lanes between the trees, beneath incessant birdsong, before heading over to the Palace Museum, the modest former residence of Sheikh Zayed—a complex of atmospheric courtyards and airy reception rooms that forms an outpost of the nearby National Museum, itself an absorbing showcase of al-Ain's Bronze and Iron Age past.

A guidebook mentioned the camel market, but of the half-dozen taxi drivers I asked—every one an Afghan; I suspected there was a cartel operating—none knew the way. I eventually found Saeed (also Afghan) who took me there. Splendid beasts from as far away as Khartoum and Karachi were going for prices topping £10,000. As we walked around the dusty pens, we saw two Emirati men in immaculate white robes, squatting in the shade of their four-wheel-drives. The photographer friend I'd hooked up with shot a couple of frames from a distance, and one of the men called us over. With a frown he asked, "Why are you taking pictures? Why do you want to make fun of us?"

I squirmed, but my friend—who is not the shy and retiring type—shouldered his camera and leaned on the car. "Why do you suppose I'm making fun of you?" he said. "People in my country have never heard of al-Ain. They want to see how you live. This," he gestured around, "is your culture. Aren't you proud of it?"

Genial, if heated, debate followed. We parted company with the men amicably, but it was a sobering exchange—not least because it threw the Gulf's cultural shifts into embarrassingly sharp relief. Ali, a market hanger-on who had attached himself to us, summed it up well. "Some people in Europe and America laugh at us because they don't understand us," he said. "This *is* our culture, and we *are* proud [of it]—but having tourists around makes things complicated."

* * *

The Liwa oasis, 150 kilometres southwest of Abu Dhabi, marks the edge of the immense Empty Quarter. I rented a car to get there. It was a superb drive, heading south on a broad highway out of the bleached, greyish landscape of the coastal *sabkha* (salt flats) and into warmer desert shades of orange and ochre.

Liwa comprises about fifty villages strung together along a hundred-kilometre arc at the limit of the dunes. It is the ancestral home of both the Al Nahyan family, rulers of Abu Dhabi, and the Al Maktoum, rulers of Dubai. Like al-Ain, it long predates the UAE's megalopolitan ambitions. In 1793, following the discovery of fresh water by a hunting party tracking gazelle on a coastal island, the al-Nahyan moved their power base there from Liwa, naming their new home *Abu Dhabi* (idiomatically, "The one with the gazelles").

Liwa remained isolated. When Wilfred Thesiger came through in 1948, he was the first European to do so. I passed the wells of Qutof, where Thesiger camped—still crowded with date palms—before heading out on what must be the greatest desert drive achievable in a rented saloon anywhere in the world. A tarmac road heads south from Liwa for twenty-five kilometres into the sands, crossing vast plains of *sabkha* flanked by dunes the colour of apricot and brown sugar. It was laid to reach Tal Moreb ("Scary Hill"), a ridge of sand three hundred metres high that is now a centre for weekend offroading. The epic scenery on the way knocked the main attraction into a cocked hat.

At the Liwa Hotel, a locally run four-star, reception staff told me about the camel fair recently held nearby. A village farmer had taken one of the top prizes. I wondered if I might meet him. Half a dozen phone calls later, and I had directions to Rashad Ali al-Mansouri's farm.

Modest and taciturn, Rashad Ali received me with grace, serving dates, spiced coffee and sweet ginger tea before taking me out to the paddocks. A dozen camels loped over in greeting. He grinned, patting one, chucking another under the chin. Then we caught sight of the champ, draped in her winning silks. Even to my untrained eye, al-Kaida (with a K, not a Q; it means "Unique") was strikingly beautiful, with wide eyes, an elegant jawline and lusciously long legs.

Rashad Ali and I stood together, leaning on a gate, and could have been in Derbyshire, our feet on muddy turf, gazing over a green valley—yet this particular dale was waterless and the hillsides were naked sand. All it took was a shift in colour to jump from England to Arabia, and I played the trick in my mind—seeing ochre, then flicking a mental switch to see green.

I explained the thought to him, but he'd never seen a green valley, so just nodded.

Then, of course, he invited me to eat with him, so we sat out on cushions after sunset and dined *al fresco*. After coffee, and his unpleasant judgements about Dubai, I wondered if he'd ever travelled.

"I went to Cairo once," he mused. "It was... alright."

He paused again, and the evening breeze brought us a few grains of sand, swirling in the dusk. "But I missed the desert," he said, and offered me more dates.

Whatever may be happening on the coast, Emirati culture is alive and well in the oases.

UAE: THE CHURCHES OF DUBAI

Religion & society / 2015 / BBC

F ather Matthew, robed in a white and gold chasuble, turned to face his sixty-strong congregation. Middle-class fathers in plaid shirts, older matriarchs under headscarves, smart-skirted women marshalling kids and even a few muscled guys in T-shirts were scattered across thirteen rows of pews in the modern, brightly lit Roman Catholic church of St Mary.

As Father Matthew raised the Communion wine, the Muslim call to prayer started from the mosque next door.

* * *

It was a Thursday evening in Dubai after work—I'd already spotted a few yawns in the back row—and I was sitting in on Mass. Unusually, it was being conducted in Urdu.

The UAE, of which Dubai is a part, has crippling restrictions on freedom of speech. There's widespread media censorship and dozens of activists are in jail. But it also has a little-known history of religious tolerance.

In 1958 Sheikh Rashid bin Saeed Al Maktoum, father of Dubai's current ruler, permitted a Hindu temple to be built on the roof of the souk. You reach it today along a lane lined with shops selling figurines of gods and goddesses and garlands of roses and marigolds.

The only such temple in a country which now holds perhaps half a million Hindus, this little makeshift space, aromatic with sandalwood, hosts tens of thousands of worshippers each week, both Hindus and Sikhs.

Then in 1966, the year oil was discovered in Dubai, Sheikh Rashid donated a pocket of land to a Roman Catholic mission.

The city has since grown up around it, and St Mary's now stands beside a busy four-lane road in central Dubai.

Since Sunday is a working day, one idiosyncrasy of Christian worship here is that the main weekly services are held on a Friday, for many people their only day off. Churches—including St Mary's—host dozens of services, in English and Arabic but also languages from Tagalog to Malayalam.

"We see seven thousand people for Friday Mass," Father Lennie Connully, St Mary's parish priest, told me.

Father Lennie couldn't put a number on Dubai's Catholics, who originate mainly from India and the Philippines. But he was clear about what Dubai offers.

"We did not expect such freedom," he told me. "But in this compound we are free to exercise our religious practices."

That's an important qualification. As you move around Dubai, you see no evidence of religion other than Islam. Churches cannot display crosses, and those who preach publicly or try to persuade Muslims to convert can expect jail and deportation.

As my Urdu Mass ended, I met Jerry Robert, the president of Dubai's Pakistani Catholic community. Originally from Karachi, Robert, tall and confident in a business suit, has been here for seventeen years. He's a bank security manager. With Christians of all denominations in Pakistan suffering violent attacks and church-burnings, I asked him about conditions in Dubai.

"Much, much better," he said. "We have freedom in a Muslim country. It's a very safe environment for us. This is what we need in Pakistan."

❋ ❋ ❋

Dubai's Protestant church Holy Trinity stands within another high-walled compound beside St Mary's, also built on land donated by Sheikh Rashid. Friday mornings see thousands of people—of mainly African and South Asian origin—attending dozens of services that run simultaneously in several chapels and prayer halls. From a packed Revivalist gathering—lots of loud music, arm-waving and "Satan get back!"—I joined an Anglican communion, traditional hymns mumbled over a funereal electric organ. I also squeezed into a Hindi Fellowship service and peeked into the Korean church as teenagers belted out Christian rock songs.

Up a double flight of stone steps, the Coptic church was full of people and incense smoke, a red-carpeted room with carved pews, panelled walls and a huge image of Christ painted on the blue ceiling. Cymbals clashed and triangles tinkled as translations of the chanted prayers flowed across two screens in both Arabic and Coptic.

Copts, the largest religious minority in Egypt, face discrimination at home and often violent attacks. Ten thousand or more live in the UAE, and young, bearded priest Father Markos, twelve years in Dubai, told me his flock are "more than happy—they enjoy their life, they are free."

A bystander from the congregation grabbed my hand.

"Life is much, much better than in Egypt," he said. "If you respect the law here, it's OK. There, if they know you're Coptic..." And he grimaced.

There are more churches across Dubai and the UAE, including several—and another Sikh *gurdwara*—on land donated by the current ruler, Sheikh Mohammed. Dubai's record on human rights and political freedom may be miserable, but this strange city remains, for some, a haven of religious tolerance.

PALESTINE-ISRAEL: BREAKING BREAD

Travel / 2014 / The Times

It was a turnip.

"…As you can see, the ladies are using this kind of, er, round radish," Ehab, the guide, was saying. I glanced at the tour group around me—Americans, Swedes, Germans. They were all nodding.

I let Ehab finish, then took him to one side.

"It's a turnip," I said.

"I think it's some kind of white beetroot," he said. "It grows in the ground."

You can't blame him. In the Middle East I've only ever seen turnips served sliced and pickled as a rarely-sampled table garnish. But here, in a vaulted Ottoman kitchen in the Palestinian city of Nablus, half a dozen local women were unmistakably preparing whole stuffed turnips for lunch.

As we prepared to start peeling and coring, Ehab opened his iPad, asked me to type "T-U-R-N-I-P" into Wikipedia, then sat in the corner scrolling and tapping. Meanwhile, I tweeted a Lebanese chef friend of mine in London, Anissa Helou, who's written widely on Middle East food. She'd also never heard of stuffed turnips. "Palestinian cuisine is very interesting," she tweeted back.

It is. And, for obvious reasons to do with conflict and political isolation, it remains mostly unknown outside the towns and villages from where it originates. You could count on one hand the number of companies taking tourists into the West Bank—and they all have political axes to grind.

Breaking Bread Journeys, a new Palestinian and Israeli joint initiative, is trying to be different. Its purpose is explicitly non-political. The founders—Elisa Moed, who is Israeli, and Christina Samara, who is Palestinian—both already run their own mainstream tour companies. They met in 2010 during discussions on tourism development brokered by Tony Blair's Quartet peace talks. Realising that they shared perspectives, the two women decided to work together.

They drew up a series of itineraries that—uniquely—cross back and forth between Israeli and Palestinian destinations, linking sites and experiences normally shut off from each other. Their project has just launched with a food tour. Hence the turnips.

Having trotted through Nablus souk buying spices and sampling deep-fried pastries in syrup ("Healthy food!" grinned the vendor), we'd ended up at a local women's project named Beit al-Karama, the House of Dignity. Its director, Fatima Qadumy, explained that besides running classes in maths and English and supporting women's empowerment, Beit al-Karama is also the sole Palestinian link to the worldwide Slow Food movement, working to preserve and document the region's culinary traditions.

That said, there was nothing slow about the way these ladies were coring turnips, deftly stuffing each with a mixture of rice and meat seasoned with cinnamon. Flash-fried to seal their outsides, the turnips then stewed in a thick sesame broth before being turned out into Armenian-style blue-and-white serving dishes. Their peppery-sweet tang, set off by the gooily aromatic rice stuffing, was lifted deliciously by lemon-scented lentil soup, crisp rocket salad and fresh-baked flat bread. We were light on leftovers.

All next day was spent roaming the alleyways of Jerusalem's Old City in the company of the Chefs For Peace, a group of Christian, Jewish and Muslim chefs who volunteer their time to promote cross-cultural cooking. As we shouldered a path through Jerusalem's markets, sampling sweet sesame *halawa* and pausing for a plate of *hummus*, the group's founder Kevork Alemian explained how a distrust of politicians sparked the idea to lead by example.

"We are simple people," he said. "When we unite in a kitchen, we forget about our differences."

The evening peaked at Bulghourji, a splendid Armenian restaurant tucked beside Jerusalem's sixteenth-century walls, discussing techniques and recipes in the kitchen, then sitting together for a heavenly spread of Levantine comfort food, pastries of melting goat cheese jostling for attention with delicately spiced ground lamb *kubbeh*.

Crucially, Breaking Bread also showcases cooking where it matters: in the home. Among glass-fronted bookcases and prints of domed skylines in her sitting room in the Jerusalem suburb of Beit Safafa, Iman Abuseir told us her family's story of exile in the 1930s and 40s from their home—now in Israel—before serving us soup of green wheat, stuffed cauliflower leaves and the classic Palestinian dish *musakhan*, chicken flavoured with pine-nuts and the lemony spice sumac.

Then in her West Jerusalem apartment of sideboards and willow prints, Ahuva Guterman—an ultra-Orthodox Jewish great-grandmother—made a blessing over dough as she encouraged us to knead our own plaited loaves of *challah*, a sweet white bread served for the ritual Friday night meal. Wreathed in baking smells, Ahuva then smilingly told us of her parents' experience of antisemitism in 1930s' Poland and their self-imposed exile to Palestine.

As throughout, we were left to draw our own conclusions. Personally, I would have preferred a bit more politics on the tour. Without context, there's always a danger you end up suggesting that quality of life and opportunities for Palestinians and Israelis are equal, which they're not.

But food and ideology rarely mix well, and this is definitely a trip for pragmatists, making linkages between cultures that neither side likes to acknowledge. It leaves you feeling that the physical barriers restricting travel in the Middle East are insignificant, compared with the mental ones.

PALESTINE: WANDERING THE WEST BANK

Travel / 2012 / Wanderlust

*I managed to persuade Wanderlust, a monthly travel maga-
zine, to commission me to write two long-form travel pieces
targeted at independent travellers seeking ideas for places to
visit, one on Palestine, one on Israel. To Wanderlust's credit,
they ran them in consecutive issues. This is the Palestine one;
the Israel one follows next.*

"I love planes!"

Lights twinkled on wingtips overhead, on the
barbed-wire fence opposite, and in Sami's eyes
beside me. A roar reached our ears, as the unseen aircraft
continued its climb into cool blackness westwards towards the Med.

Sami chuckled. "But do you know what I love even
more?" He tilted his beer bottle again. "Helicopters.

Once, I managed to get out, and flew to see my cousin. Dubai-Singapore-Melbourne. Then I paid a hundred dollars for a ten-minute ride in a helicopter. Whoo!"

I grinned with him as he punched the air, remembering.

"We don't have the opportunity for that in Palestine," he laughed.

Yes, he said Palestine. Relax. Here, have a beer. Have some of Sami's Japanese rice crackers. This is *Wanderlust*, not *World's Most Dangerous Hotspots*. Palestine really is a viable travel destination.

First, some definitions. Palestine, for the purposes of this article, means the West Bank, a kidney-shaped chunk of hilly terrain stretching north and south of Jerusalem. (Gaza, the other bit of Palestine away on the Mediterranean coast, remains off-limits to tourists.) I'll spare you the history lesson, but present-day reality is that the West Bank is under Israeli military occupation. International law calls the occupation illegal; Israel disputes that.

What the occupation means for travellers is, in effect, two countries overlaid on top of each another. Distances are small—barely eight kilometres separate Jerusalem and Bethlehem, while Ramallah to Nablus is only thirty-five kilometres—but Israeli army checkpoints across every major route, and at the entrance to every Palestinian town, can lengthen travel times. "Settlers"—that is, Israelis who reside in the West Bank—live entirely separately from Palestinians, supported by their government and guarded by their army. They have their own towns (or "settlements") which are secured against outsiders, their own infrastructure of water and utilities, their own bus network and even their own roads, along which Palestinians may not drive.

Sami's balcony—in Beit Sahour, on the edge of Bethlehem—gives an eagle-eye view over one of those settlements, a high-density cluster of identikit red-roofed new builds. I'd seen the same place the night before, when I'd sat down for hummus and kebabs with George Rishmawi, coordinating guide for the Siraj Center, a non-profit organisation working in sustainable tourism. As we looked out over purple Beit Sahour, with its dim streetlights and patches of shadow, George pointed north to the settlement, floodlit yellow.

"Har Homa," he said. "Built on our land. That hill has been called Jabal Abu Ghneim since..." He waved his hand. "Stolen."

It was Har Homa that glowered opposite Sami's balcony, too.

✱ ✱ ✱

With the physique of a bodybuilder and a handshake to match, my homestay host Sami Khair turned out to be—would I make this up?—a carpenter in Bethlehem. Crafted wood filled his family's modestly-sized villa, from the super-sleek kitchen island unit to the featherlight dining table and wall-hung crucifix. While Sami showed me around, six-year-old Fernando consoled himself with a bout of American wrestling on the TV, gutted that the Premier League football stickers I'd brought from England didn't include his namesake Fernando Torres.

Sami's wife Iman, a special-needs teacher, laid out a feast of chicken, salad, fresh bread and mint tea, and we chatted about travel, work, family—all refreshingly ordinary. Fernando took the insult of being kicked out of his room remarkably well, considering the sticker thing: he showed me his ninja moves, explained how the light worked and then scampered off to his sisters' room, where he was extravagantly shushed while Sami and I watched planes.

My Bethlehem guide was Rafat Salsa, once a Communist, now, intriguingly, a factory owner. As we drove into town next morning, he explained in detail how he was handling delicate negotiations that week with a Italian firm for a huge order of Christian religious artefacts and nativity scenes, carved in local olive wood and stamped 'Made In Bethlehem'. "Every rosary I sell, twenty-five families benefit," he said.

In Bethlehem's big Manger Square, Israeli tour buses were disgorging daytrippers onto the flagstones for what is many people's one and only experience of Palestine—a visit to the ancient, rambling Church of the Nativity, reputed site of Jesus's birth.

Rafat gave me a look. "The guides don't even tell them they're not in Israel anymore," he said.

We waited our turn to duck through the Door of Humility, a chest-high opening that is now the church's main entrance, after Crusaders and then Ottomans blocked the portal to halt cavalry charges. But if Rafat had prepared some historical patter he didn't let on: we were neither of us really in the mood to linger. I knew from previous visits that the time to see this magnificent church is early. Now, in the middle of the day, the altar steps leading down to the grotto where Jesus was born were like a tube station on a strike day. Rafat had a word with the duty police officer, and motioned me to slip down the up stairs instead.

In the crypt among grappling shadows, I wedged my back into an airless corner to watch tides of individuals prostrate themselves—on knees, elbows, even full-length on the floor—before an 18th-century silver star, set within a low alcove at the supposed location of Christ's birth. Candles sputtered, lips mumbled, hot sweat pooled in my collarbones. It was a claustrophobe's agony.

Truth to tell, I was less engaged by the Holy Land's standard tourist narrative of pilgrimage and history than by its contemporary vim. I enjoyed chitchatting with sellers of beachballs and cheap shoes in Bethlehem's souk more than the church. It was the same in Jerusalem, where veteran guide Mohammed Barakat lifted a walk along the Via Dolorosa with tales of his family's past among the Old City's courtyards. And again an hour north in Ramallah, where the streets buzzed with commerce and a sashed soldier raised his chin over Yasser Arafat's kitschly sombre tomb.

Twenty kilometres south of Bethlehem within Hebron's medieval souk, as beautiful as Jerusalem's, where Jewish settlers in fortified encampments on the rooftops toss dead rats and dirty nappies onto the heads of Palestinian passers-by, I was stopped at a caged-in checkpoint.

"Why are you here?" I asked the Israeli sentry.

He shifted his automatic weapon. "To protect life."

"Whose life are you protecting?" I asked.

A second passed. "Mine," he said.

I almost laughed. Then I nearly cried.

One morning in Bethlehem I took a walk to Israel's infamous Separation Wall. Eight metres high, punctuated by blank-eyed watchtowers, it coils around the city's northern extremity like a concrete garrotte, severing the road to Jerusalem. Here, as across the West Bank, the Israeli army controls Palestinians' movement. Many people cannot enter Jerusalem at all. Israel calls it a security measure.

To offset the wall's greyness, countless well-meaning hands have left acres of graffiti—glib images of freedom I knew I should like, and even glibber multilingual slogans. Past a Banksy dove I approached the Aida refugee camp—in effect a cramped, poorly supplied, low-income housing estate—crunched tight up against the painted wall.

Built in 1950 for five hundred refugees displaced from their homes in the new State of Israel, Aida now houses five thousand people, two-thirds of them under the age of eighteen. It isn't the best-known of Bethlehem's refugee camps—Deheishe, further south, has a café, shop and guesthouse—but in Aida I was keen to meet Abdelfattah Abusrour. A saturnine forty-something, biologist Abusrour gave up a university teaching position in France to launch al-Rowwad, a theatre project for Aida's children. In his office under photos of Gandhi, Einstein, Mother Teresa and Martin Luther King, he explained his idea of "Beautiful Resistance", bringing purpose to lives blighted by political uncertainty.

"We're fed up of walking in the funerals of our children," he said. "My intent is to make everybody here feel they can be a changemaker. Theatre can be one of the most powerful civilising forces of resistance."

I started talking about Israel's wall, which was visible through the office window—but Abusrour stopped my question with a tut.

"Artists come and turn this wall into a museum. Then people admire it." He shook his head. "The wall is illegal and ugly. It should remain illegal and ugly."

* * *

Next day George Rishmawi took me on a long drive through the Jerusalem Wilderness—the Palestinian term for the deserts of Judea—on a looping route from leafy Beit Sahour down through an immense landscape of dimpled nakedness into Wadi Nar (the "Valley of Fire"). Low-impact tourism is just opening up here, centred on desert hikes and Bedouin-hosted camping in the Dead Sea hills. I was interested in the Wadi Qelt trail. This arduous twenty-five-kilometre canyon hike drops from 640 metres above sea level near Jerusalem to 250 metres below sea level at Jericho. George proposed the final stage, and our three-hour descent began on the steep approach to St George's Monastery, founded in the fourth century over a cave where Elijah was purportedly fed by ravens in the desert (though in Hebrew 'ravens' is virtually identical to 'Arabs'—was it a miracle, or just a spelling mistake?). Glued onto the canyon's north face, the monastery's sunlit steeples turned out to shelter only a couple of monkish sourpusses, who showed us the gloomy nineteenth-century chapel, the cold-water tap— and the donations box.

Then it was just our bootsteps as the velvet heat deepened around us. A spooked dog sent barks ricocheting around the canyon. Down in Jericho, midday at virtually the lowest point on Earth was like being basted in clingfilm. The sweat wouldn't stop. I glistened as we rode a little cable car above banana plantations, and I dripped onto the gorgeous early-Islamic mosaics at Hisham's Palace.

Salvation came via the Tariq al-Mu'arrajat ("Road of Curves"), perhaps Palestine's most scenic drive, coiling from Jericho's deserts for an hour or so up to the green lanes of Taybeh, where George made straight for the most aromatic building in town.

Taybeh Beer, the Arab world's one and only micro-brewery, spreads a luscious scent—malty, yeasty, fruity, hoppy—over this highland village's olive-laden slopes. Brewmaster Madees Khoury showed us round, explaining the brewing process as the sunshine slanted lower. Aged only 26, she came to work with her father at the brewery after graduating from Bir Zeit University nearby.

"We're here to stay," she grinned. "We're making a quality product, using local spring water, following German purity laws. It's one hundred percent natural." Thirsty travellers toasted success.

*　*　*

Thirty kilometres north, across hills of figs, olives and settlements, morning broke in Nablus—a mountain-flanked city of 180,000 people—to birdsong. A cock crowed, a bell chimed, keys hit a lock. In the church at Jacob's Well, a Spanish prayer group chanted as they drew water.

The day began with a speed-walk through the Nablus souk, peeking into a traditional olive-oil soap factory and scoffing plates of knafeh, a classic dessert of buttery semolina, goat cheese and sugar syrup—and it ended at Sebastia, a Roman city crumbling atop wooded hills nearby, where shopowner Mahmoud Ghazal showed me shelves full of unsold millennium memorabilia. Nobody had visited from 2000 until 2011, he said, pouring me tea with a smile. Nobody.

There's a word in Arabic, *sumud*. It's difficult to translate—take a look at its Wikipedia page for clues—but it means something like resilience, or steadfastness. Palestinians have *sumud* in spades. You see it everywhere, that quiet patience: this is the land of the long view. Visiting isn't about ticking off places and, perhaps contrary to expectation, it isn't really about politics either. It's about the cast of characters, and their *sumud*. My week in Palestine was full of people, of talking, exchanging stories, overturning preconceptions. Everybody had a tale to tell. Time was on our side. It was good travel.

ISRAEL: TOUGH ON THE OUTSIDE

Travel / 2012 / Wanderlust

I managed to persuade Wanderlust, a monthly travel maga-
zine, to commission me to write two long-form travel pieces
targeted at independent travellers seeking ideas for places to
visit, one on Palestine, one on Israel. To Wanderlust's credit,
they ran them in consecutive issues. This is the Israel one; the
Palestine one comes previously.

Rapture. The end of days. The seven seals. The four horsemen of the apocalypse.

You have to believe me, I really tried. I paced. I squinted. I did my level best to summon up the fury and the chaos of the final, tumultuous battle to come between divine forces of good and evil. But standing in the morning sunshine at Har Megiddo—translated in the Book of Revelation as "Armageddon"—the only thing I could summon up was a scarlet Coke lorry, rumbling past on Highway 65 towards the coast.

Beyond the ruin-speckled slopes (Megiddo was a biblical metropolis), fields spruced the broad Jezreel Valley
in blissful green. The air tasted of pomegranates. I pondered Satanic majesty as birds chirruped for joy. I wres-
tled the Antichrist while dappled shadows played on pitted stonework.

All in vain. Armageddon was delightful. It just made
me cross with frustration.

That's Israel all over—visually stunning, but pre-
loaded with so much baggage the simplest excursion
takes on epic profundity. It's like the most mesmerising
of the God channels on TV: the sheer emotional pitch of
the place means every mundane minute of every ordinary day rings with exhausting intensity. Each stone has
significance.

Israel—a sliver on the eastern Med—was declared a
state in 1948 during a conflict the Israelis term the
War of Independence (Palestinians, bereaved, expelled,
dispossessed, call it "The Catastrophe"). In last month's
Wanderlust I wrote about getting off the beaten track in
the West Bank, a chunk of land that has been occupied by
Israel since 1967. This month the focus is Israel "proper",
within its 1948 borders.

Roughly half of that land area is taken up by the
Negev desert. Outside a small town near Jerusalem, I
met guide Amir Gadnaor for the journey into the Negev.
Straggle-bearded, floppy-hatted and—when he slid his
wraparound sunglasses up—crinkle-eyed, Amir lives in
Shaharut, a bone-dry huddle of houses on an arid clifftop
near Eilat, some three hundred kilometres to the south.
For him, this was the long drive home.

Charmingly, "tour guide" in Hebrew is *moreh derekh*, a
teacher of the road. Amir fulfilled the brief literally and

metaphorically, steering southwards as the land dried around us from green to ochre, while pointing out drip-irrigated fields and copses created by terracing on the dry hills. "In 1948 this was desert," he said, in an echo of the falsehoods promulgated by early Zionist settlers in Palestine. "Now, it's the breadbasket of Israel."

But, he added, there's been a cost. For thousands of years the bedouin roamed freely across the borderless deserts between Egypt and Arabia. Then 1948 severed links. Many families caught in the middle—that is, in the Negev—were expelled. The remainder who stayed were concentrated by the new Israeli government into a shard of land around the desert frontier city of Beersheva, then ignored. To this day tens of thousands of people remain trapped in "unrecognised" villages in the Negev—communities which don't officially exist, lacking access to services or utilities.

We followed an unsigned track to one, set between stony slopes. Amir told me it was called Arika. He wanted me to meet a bedouin friend of his, Yusef, who could explain more—but when we arrived Yusef was away. Amir and I reclined on cushions in the family tent, open to the breeze on both sides, while the kids kicked a ball outside. One of the ladies of the family poured glasses of sweet tea before retiring discreetly. There was no opportunity to chat. It was awkward. The bedouin are the most hospitable people I know, and will bend over backwards to make any guest feel welcome. Presumably Amir knew this family, and they knew him. Nevertheless, he and I sipped and left.

Further south, where the panorama of naked peaks looked like a rumpled tablecloth, Amir pointed out a green-speckled wadi, centrepiece of the Ein Avdat National Park. Down on the desert floor, the heat was magnificent, welcoming, uplifting. We crunched into the canyon and my eyes skated over the striated walls, bleached white limestone supported on reddish and greenish clays and laced with blackish seams of flint. Mossy pools flanked by tamarisk reflected a dragonfly's escape into high shadow.

At the head of the wadi, Amir showed me a caper plant. I watched him explain how it keeps its leaf surface salty, to osmotically suck moisture from the air, and how its seeds are slightly acidic, so if they fall on limestone they dissolve it a little to attach more firmly.

"The desert can give you a lot of strength, if you let it," he murmured philosophically, before straightening up.

The rest of the day I remained the pupil to Amir's *moreh derekh*—at the majestic hilltop ruins of Avdat, a frankincense trading station on the camel-caravan route between Petra and the coast; at the Ramon Crater, a vast, eroded desert depression; at an isolated alpaca farm, where horse-riders were setting off to view the sunset.

When we reached Shaharut, Amir refused to let me sleep alone in the tourist cabin beside the village and instead welcomed me into his family home, a large caravan that he had anchored and rendered in adobe.

"We came to Shaharut twenty-one years ago," he told me that night, adding wood to the fire and giving the pot a stir. "It's a very hard place to live; if you don't enjoy the hardship you won't make it. The first thing people do when they come to the desert is try to change it." He shook his head. "Then it changes them."

* * *

Next day was focused around Kibbutz Lotan, one of the Negev's string of "intentional communities". Now a centre for ecotourism and birdwatching, Lotan retains its commitment to the liberal Jewish ideal of *tikkun olam*, or repairing the world. It has a Centre for Creative Ecology, domed adobe huts formed from bentonite, a clay-like industrial by-product. There's a kids' eco-education zone. They recycle, they have composting toilets, they keep goats for yoghurt and they produce a thousand tonnes of dates a year.

But Amir's words about changing the desert kept ringing in my head. Around the Negev I kept finding new-agey tourist camps, idealistic collectives, organic farm shops, even a desert ashram. Timna, a centre for copper-mining under the ancient Egyptians 3,500 years ago, hosted fabulous rock formations—pillars, bulbous mushrooms, vast canyons—but it was empty. Walking between rock walls, eroded like melting candle-wax, I thought of the same landscapes a few miles east around Wadi Rum in Jordan, and how little they would mean if they, too, had been emptied of the bedouin.

The memory of this absence survives in Hebrew. The word for desert, *midbar*, derives from *lehadbir*, meaning a grazing-place. The Negev was always a human landscape. Peopled. Now almost ninety percent of it is given over to army bases and aerial bombing ranges. The remainder is dominated by urban preoccupations and intensive agriculture.

It's like the Highland Clearances. Who's left to graze?

Timna is just about the saddest place I know.

* * *

I headed north to blow the cobwebs away.

After Tel Aviv—a whirl of Bauhaus architecture, ethnic food and fashionable people—a shore-hugging train ride led in half an hour to Zikhron Yaakov. One of the oldest of modern Israel's new towns, Zikhron was founded in 1882 on forested hilltops beside what was the Palestinian village of Zammarin. Zammarin has long since disappeared, subsumed by its neighbour. Bougainvillea drenches the shaded porches, wooden fences and red tiled roofs of Zikhron's nineteenth-century villas. Arched alleys hide ochre-painted jewellery shops and craft galleries. It's an effortless place. Israelis weekend there in droves.

On the cobbled main street sassy tweens speed-walked together towards a pink ice-cream parlour. Spreading around a hidden courtyard I found Tut Neyar, Israel's only handmade paper workshop. Owner Timna Neumann sat with me under the shade of a mulberry tree while three Israeli visitors turned mulberry bark into paper—pulping, draining, pressing. We chatted. We chewed sugar-cane. We let shadows lengthen. Artisan papermaking suits Zikhron perfectly.

Grapes have been a big success. One side of town is fragrant from the Carmel winery. At a wine bar-cum-deli run by Tishbi, another estate vineyard, a rather nice Merlot accompanied a platter of distinctly upmarket "Israeli mezze" (ciabatta, black olive paste, roasted peppers—the "Israeli" tag was baffling).

Across town Nachi Bargida, whose Romanian great-great-grandfather was one of the first new arrivals in Zikhron, in 1887, clinked pilsner glasses while explaining the story of his newly-opened microbrewery. "I wanted to do something to make people happy," Nachi said. "We are not only holy sites, not only the Arab-Israeli conflict. We're living a great life, having a great time." To our left the sun was kissing the Med. To our right hills rolled towards Armageddon. Nachi spread his arms. "The width of Israel!" he laughed. I wondered if it was a toast.

* * *

Routes from Zikhron usually point north to the port city of Haifa, or west to the coast for historic Caesarea and Acre. I went the other way. Twenty minutes east in the town of Umm al-Fahem, Said Abu Shakra took hold of my elbow. "I'm trying to paint myself out of a corner," he chortled, as he walked me round his gallery.

One of the largest Palestinian towns inside Israel (population 45,000), Umm al-Fahem has a reputation for hostility: you won't find it in the official tourist literature. In truth, it's perfectly ordinary. Its best restaurant, El Babur, serves rustic Lebanese-style food as good as any I've tasted in the entire Middle East. And in an unremarkable town house, stocky ex-police officer Abu Shakra has defied expectations to open the first Palestinian gallery of contemporary art in the country.

"People come here just to shake hands and discover a genuine side of Palestinian life," he told me. By building bridges with the initially wary municipality, holding film screenings for local schools, running art therapy classes and offering free workshops for children with disabilities, Abu Shakra—an art-school graduate himself— has changed his home town. Local artists exhibit alongside international stars, drawing Palestinian and Jewish Israeli enthusiasts alike. "Crazy people like me want to create dialogue," he grinned.

That desire for dialogue extends to tourism. In 2008 US outdoor adventure specialists David and Anna Landis and Israeli tourism entrepreneur Maoz Inon created the Jesus Trail, a sixty-five-kilometre route linking Nazareth—the town where Jesus grew up—to sites of pilgrimage around the Sea of Galilee. Uniquely, it combines Christian and Jewish sites with Muslim and Druze holy places that lie well beyond standard tour itineraries. It was a labour of love: the trail is free, public and non-profit, feeding visitors (and, therefore, money) into rural communities along the way.

I met the founders at the Fauzi Azar Inn, in the Old City lanes of Nazareth. A global winner at last year's Responsible Tourism Awards, this remarkable small hotel—a nineteenth-century Ottoman mansion of arches, frescoes and painted ceilings—lay empty after the death in 1980 of its owner, Palestinian businessman Fauzi Azar. Revamped as an inn by Maoz in 2005, it has transformed its neighbourhood. Restaurants, hotels and shops are thriving. Nazareth's mayor is getting involved. And from the beginning the Azar family have remained partners: today Fauzi Azar's granddaughter, Suraida Nasser, manages this cross-cultural enterprise in the house she remembers as a child.

Appropriately, the Jesus Trail passes the inn's door. I walked parts of Stage 1, taking in the spectacular Roman-Byzantine mosaics at Zippori, but David and Anna were keen to show me some scenery. We fast-forwarded thirty kilometres or so east to Stage 6 and the gentle ascent of Mount Arbel, where suddenly a panorama opened up across the entire, teardrop-blue Sea of Galilee, clear to Syria and Jordan. Memorable scrambling followed, on rocky paths leading down Arbel's four-hundred-metre cliffs, before the sun set theatrically behind the twin-peaked Horns of Hattin, location of Salah ad-Din's victory over the Crusaders in 1187.

Sabra in Hebrew means a cactus fruit—prickly on the outside, sweet in the middle. It's also the word used to describe a native-born Israeli. The metaphor fits like a glove: this is avowedly not a land of social graces, but once you learn how to unpeel the brusqueness, there's generally kindness and generosity beneath. People might even smile.

Yet in tourism terms, it's almost as if the *sabra* has been turned inside out. Travel is easy here: everything works, the landscapes astound, there's history galore and it all slots into a ready-made narrative. It's when you try to dig down that you encounter the prickles of competing histories, untold stories and forgotten—or, indeed, deliberately erased—places. Israel makes for fascinating, depressing, inspiring, confusing travel. Come prepared.

PALESTINE: TO ROAM AT WILL

Culture & society / 2018 / AramcoWorld

I t's a torrent of teenagers, flowing uphill towards me on a narrow trail. I step to the left, cramming myself into a wedge of stone wall beneath the spread of an olive tree as they clatter past in a cloud of bubblegum perfume, sullen-eyed puffing, laughter and primary colours. The last in line gives me side-eye as he shoulders an outsized loudspeaker up towards the trailhead on the slopes above.

Salvation awaited him just above in Battir, a village lining a curve of terraced hills a few kilometres southwest of Jerusalem. After drinks and snacks there, he would join the rest of his fellow students on a bus back to their home city of Ramallah.

"These rural trails are fun, but they're also enriching our Palestinian identity," observed Battir café-owner Hassan Muammar, after they'd gone.

Earlier, on the opposite, eastern side of Jerusalem, I spent most of a day with the serene crunch of my own bootsteps on a dry trail that echoed down through the Wadi Qelt canyon. Velvet heat rose in waves. At the end, the palm trees of Jericho appeared through salty lashes like cocktail umbrellas, stuck into liquid heat-haze on the floor of the desert.

"Walking like this makes a new connection to Palestine. Your belonging becomes less poetic and more concrete," said Rosann, a local college graduate.

Palestinians have always walked the land. But now, unexpectedly, walking is changing how many Palestinians feel about the land.

"The previous generation—I'm talking about the 1930s and 1940s—they were out there walking, especially Wadi Qelt in spring, when everywhere is filled with flowers," says Ali Qleibo, professor of anthropology at Jerusalem's Al Quds University.

"We see them in old pictures. This is part of the foundation of the Palestinian identity."

But even earlier, when walking was a necessity for the lack of transport (other than four-legged varieties), there was still a tradition of hiking for pleasure. Qleibo mentions the writer Raja Shehadeh, who described the concept of *sarha*:

"It was mainly young men who went on these expeditions. They would take a few provisions and go to the open hills, disappear for the whole day, sometimes for weeks and months. They often didn't have a particular destination. To go on a *sarha* was to roam freely, at will, without restraint," Shehadeh wrote in his 2007 book *Palestinian Walks*.

Written records of *sarhat* are rare. In 1925 two friends Nicola Ziadeh (later emeritus professor at the American University of Beirut) and Darwish Mikdadi (later

Kuwait's director of education) walked from Safad, in northern Palestine, through the mountains of Lebanon and across Syria as far as modern-day Antakya—perhaps five hundred kilometres. It took them only seventeen days, walking nine or more hours each day. "Darwish loved walking and had the patience and temperament for it, as did I," wrote Ziadeh, in his memoir of the adventure. The idea of walking for pleasure survived war and social dislocation. Shehadeh himself led walks in the hills around his home city of Ramallah in the 1980s and 90s.

But since the intensification of occupation two decades ago, checkpoints, road closures and other impediments made it difficult for Palestinians to move around the West Bank.

Horizons shrank, says tourism entrepreneur George Rishmawi. Many people lived their lives in and around their home neighbourhoods. Walking in the countryside faded from view.

"Our freedom of movement has been completely restricted. There are generations that don't know Palestine," he says.

Beside the physical blocks, there's also a mental one. Arabic has no word for hiking. Different dialects substitute their own circumlocutions, but Palestinian Arabic relies on *sarha*, which connotes wandering, or *shat'ha*, meaning an enjoyable outing, such as a picnic. Neither really fits, and an idea without a name is always hard to grasp.

Rishmawi was involved in the first of Palestine's initiatives to reintroduce the reality of long-distance walking for pleasure. In 1996, as part of "Bethlehem 2000", a UN-backed project to attract development to Palestine for celebrations around the anniversary of the birth of Jesus Christ, the Palestinian government sponsored the creation of the Nativity Trail. Developed by two tour operators, Alternative Tourism Group and Siraj Center, the trail forms a 160-kilometre walking route from Nazareth to Bethlehem, recreating the journey taken before Jesus's birth by his parents Mary and Joseph.

Rishmawi remembers the first through-walk, in December 1999: "We arrived to Manger Square in Bethlehem with three camels, a donkey and a lady on the donkey who was pregnant [representing Mary, soon-to-be mother of Jesus]," he laughs.

At that time, Palestinian walkers didn't really feature in the equation.

"The idea was to attract foreign tourists," says tour operator and walking guide Mark Khano. At Khano's invitation, two British explorers, Tony Howard and Di Taylor, walked the Nativity Trail in 2000, publishing a pioneering English-language guidebook.

"Palestine wanted products, and the Nativity Trail was one of the first ideas, linked to mass-market tourism," says Raed Saadeh, a leader in sustainable tourism development. "This sort of alternative pilgrimage attracted a lot of visitors who felt a link to Palestine. But tourism is a platform for identity. What we'd like to see is a trend towards connecting to the local community, rather than just a trend to walk."

* * *

A sunny autumn morning in Bethlehem sees municipal workers clearing leaves in Manger Square, the main public space. On the edge of a small group of fit-looking Europeans and Americans kitted out for hiking, two middle-aged Palestinian men are getting acquainted. Silver-stubbled Yusuf Salah, a few belongings clutched in a plastic bag, says he's done a bit of walking before, but never this route.

His newfound trail buddy, Hani Abu Taih, smiling under a straw hat, concurs.

"This will be my first time walking long-distance in the countryside," Abu Taih says. "Twenty years I've been walking, one or two hours every morning. But just around my village near Nazareth, and always alone. I want to try walking with a group."

Slightly removed by language and appearance from their fellow hikers—some of whom are tourists, some resident expatriates—the two pals psych themselves up for the day ahead walking the Masar Ibrahim, now the best-known of Palestine's long-distance hiking trails.

"Masar" is the Arabic word for path, and "Ibrahim" is Abraham, the founder of Judaism, Christianity, and Islam. The name translates into English as "Abraham Path".

Unlike other, ancient pilgrimage routes, the Abraham Path is a modern creation, devised in 2006 by a group from Harvard Law School in the US headed by William Ury, a specialist in negotiation strategy. Ury's idea was to help fuel cross-cultural understanding among the peoples of the Middle East—and bring transformational socio-economic benefits—through the power of the simple act of walking. Walking, as he puts it, creates the space for people to envisage fresh solutions to fixed challenges.

Abraham, the origin figure of monotheistic belief, is said to have walked with his family all across the Middle

East—from Ur, his place of birth (often identified with Ur in Iraq, but also linked with Urfa in southern Turkey), through modern-day Syria and Jordan to Palestine, where his tomb is venerated today in the city of Hebron. Further traditions place Abraham—known as "Al Khalil", "the Friend", for his embodiment of loyalty and hospitality—in Egypt and Saudi Arabia.

There is no historical evidence for Abraham's existence four thousand years ago, or for the route he might have followed. No pre-existing path links these places. All we have are stories. But by listening to local people, researchers with Ury's US-based nonprofit Abraham Path Initiative (API) were able to begin mapping the constellation of traditions, folk memories, tales and legends surrounding Abraham that suffuse the multi-ethnic cultures of the Middle East. A trending line began to emerge, connoting linkage and a shared Abrahamic heritage. From that, a physical walking route could be plotted.

For most of the last decade, API has painstakingly built local capacity along sections of that route through a loosely affiliated network of trekking scouts, community outreach volunteers and partner organisations on the ground. Today, with API stepping back from trail development to a quieter funding role, ownership of the route's active sections has passed fully to local partners.

In Jordan, for example, guides, tourism professionals and community activists built on the Abraham Path's early growth in one remote highland region to develop a full-blown national hiking project. The result was the Jordan Trail, launched in 2017 as thirty-six day walks that link together to form a six-week trekking route running 650 kilometres from one end of the country to the other.

Elsewhere, southern Turkey had 170 kilometres of Abraham Path trail open by 2012, though war in Syria cut further progress short. Specialists are currently working with API to explore trail development in Saudi Arabia. In Egypt, three bedouin tribes, backed by NGOs and local volunteers, launched the 250-kilometre Sinai Trail in 2015, leading from the Red Sea coast to the summit of Egypt's highest mountain, Jabal Katarina.

Support is shared. Partners of the Sinai Trail, beside the Jordan Trail Association, include "Masar Ibrahim Al Khalil", the Palestinian NGO that has developed API's route in the West Bank. The NGO took its name from the Arabic translation of Abraham Path. In turn, it gives its name back to the route it now manages.

That route begins at Rummana, at the northernmost limit of the West Bank near Jenin. It leads south, through the cities of Nablus, Jericho, and Bethlehem, to end among the villages south of Hebron – 330 kilometres in total, divided into twenty-one day-stages. It deliberately zigzags, to bind otherwise marginalised rural communities into what has become a national trail.

"Masar Ibrahim bypassed the old trails," says Raed Saadeh. "It is a community endeavour, built in such a way as to induce community empowerment."

It has also drawn substantial international funding: In 2014 the World Bank gave the project $2.3 million over four years. The French agency for international development AFD provided €1.4 million in 2016, and French NGOs and private-sector bodies are giving further support.

This has paid for trail development, waymarking, training for guides, ancillary support along the trail such as homestays and guest houses, a staff of ten at offices near Bethlehem, and a subsidised public programme of weekly walks. High-quality digital cartography by US trail developers David Landis and Anna Dintaman forms the basis of a detailed, informative website. Slick and effective marketing gets the word out.

Open access to the trail means gauging success is hard. Using data from partners, guides and guest house owners, George Rishmawi, executive director of the Masar Ibrahim NGO, estimates six thousand people walked the path last year. Between a half and three-quarters of them were Palestinian—some individuals, but mainly organised groups, including students and youth associations.

Rishmawi speaks passionately about the value of creating new reasons for Palestinians to visit the countryside.

"We have such a beautiful country, but it's not been utilised before for this kind of [local] tourism. This is an opportunity for people to reconcile their heritage," he says.

One of Masar Ibrahim's founding partners is the Rozana Association, set up to help overcome rural problems of economic disadvantage and loss of community. Headquartered in the country town of Birzeit, a tight tangle of cobbled lanes in the hills north of Ramallah, Rozana has facilitated architectural restoration in Birzeit itself, converting one Ottoman mansion into a science centre that draws school groups, and established an annual cultural festival that now brings 35,000 visitors to this town of around seven thousand residents.

"The question was how to strengthen this attractiveness. You need to have tourism demand, especially local," says Raed Saadeh, Rozana's founder. "So in 2008 we created the Sufi Trails. This is different from Masar Ibrahim, which is a long trail that zigzags from village to village. The Sufi Trails starts with a hub, then creates a cluster of routes to villages around that hub. Together, such a cluster should have enough resources and capacity to create a destination."

Named for Sufism, a mystical practice within Islam, the Sufi Trails form a spider's-web of generally unmarked footpaths in the northern West Bank leading to ancient shrines dedicated to local Muslim saints. Many such shrines dot the hills, once revered as pilgrimage destinations, today often half-forgotten.

"Walking helps protect this type of heritage. We source funding to preserve the shrines and make them usable by converting them into the centrepieces of small community parks. They're spiritual, sentimental places that tell stories. They become an attraction," Saadeh says.

Rozana's principle of clustering also avoids imposing external management, by combining the abilities of pre-existing community organisations. In the highland village of Deir Ghassaneh, one of Rozana's rural hubs, head of the local women's association Insaf Shuoibi spoke to me of the economic benefits that have accrued by joining forces with a neighbouring village to build capacity on their local trails.

"Five years ago it was mostly foreigners visiting, but now the word is spreading, so we have more Palestinians," she said.

Another of Masar Ibrahim's founding partners is non-profit tour operator Siraj Center. For Siraj's ebullient director Michel Awad, the last few years have seen an astonishing shift.

"People never thought of walking as a journey—it was

just a way to get from point A to point B," he says. "Now they're discovering hiking for pleasure. They're beginning to understand the beauty of this land."

Ramallah-based mountain guide Wael Haj runs Palterhal, a firm offering rural hikes and eco-retreats for companies. "Managers used to organise corporate retreats indoors, in hotels—but now they're asking us to take their staff out to small villages and into nature," Haj told me. "This makes a big change in how Palestinians see their own country."

* * *

After chatting in Bethlehem's morning sunshine, the Masar Ibrahim group that includes Yusuf Salah and Hani Abu Taih take their first steps, down the steep streets leading out of Manger Square. Their route soon leaves the city behind, passing by a spring in the hills before winding through a fertile valley to end almost five hours later in the village of Tuqua.

There, householder and construction worker Salim Saba greets the walkers, bustling them through the narrow hallway of his house and out to a shaded rear balcony, for glasses of cold juice and sweet tea.

"The walk was better than I was expecting," grins Abu Taih, looking across to the two-thousand-year-old hilltop fortress Herodium just beyond Tuqua. "The guide, the company, the landscapes—what a great opportunity to share this path."

As Saba shows the group into his dining room for a homecooked lunch of chicken, rice and salad, he tells me: "I believe in this one hundred percent. For economic reasons, it helps support my family—but I'm really enjoying it, meeting all these people."

He shows me the guest rooms he has fitted out with the help of the Masar Ibrahim NGO, which split costs with him fifty-fifty. The NGO retains ownership for five years, after which the beds and their neat branded covers become his. Then he takes me through to the half-built extra rooms he is adding to the house, to accommodate the increasing numbers of walkers passing through.

The group's Palestinian guide George Giacaman, a wiry, pencil-thin figure in Lycra who, he tells me, just came from leading a group of thirty-five Norwegians on an eleven-day trek along the Nativity Trail, is proud to be involved. "The Masar Ibrahim is especially helping women in the villages, who work at home—they make food for people walking through, or products to sell," he says.

This is a familiar model for sustainable development. Relatively small amounts of external funding spur creative input from local minds building trust and capacity, thereby helping open new markets, bringing new consumers into direct contact with rural suppliers.

Dutch economist Stefan Szepesi grasped the potential. He arrived in Palestine in 2006 to work on governmental projects with the European Union. But he had itchy feet. "I first started walking out of curiosity. What was Palestine like beyond the confined view of a diplomatic car?" he has written.

Eventually, the walking took over. Szepesi switched jobs to become executive director of API, working with the Masar Ibrahim NGO and others. He also published a thick, full-colour guidebook of walks around the West Bank.

But, as he readily acknowledges, English-language

books have a limited local readership, and foreign tourism is simply not big enough in Palestine to deliver sustainable growth. It's social media that has finally brought walking into the Palestinian mainstream. Over the last ten years or so, outdoors enthusiasts have created dozens, maybe hundreds, of online and email groups where like-minded people can share information on routes and publicise excursions and weekend hikes. Szepesi's "Walking Palestine" Facebook group was one of the first, alongside others created by students in Ramallah, Nablus and elsewhere. Szepesi has stepped back from active involvement but "Walking Palestine" continues, now with almost five thousand members.

"Walking didn't happen until it became formalised, thanks partly to the work of Stefan Szepesi," says Ihab Jabari, director of the Holy Land Incoming Tour Operators' Association. "I've just done Wadi Qelt with my kids. This is so new for us, as families. It gives you a sense of belonging again."

Seeing shared images posted by local walkers out in the countryside, and hearing their first-hand accounts, has brought a fresh sense of scale, immediacy, and possibility, says Walking Palestine's current moderator, Simon Jaser.

"It's the 35 to 55 demographic who are really into walking—these are professional people," he says.

Sharing tea at one of Ramallah's busy sidewalk cafés, Jaser tells me he has covered most of the West Bank on foot.

"First I study Google Earth to find possible trails. Then I try to do experimental hikes on my own before I bring people out. Every Sunday, I take a taxi somewhere and walk into the hills."

Beside working part-time as a consular official, Jaser is a successful independent guide, careful to channel some of his profits back into rural communities, but he also offers his services for free. Each weekend he advertises a walk via Walking Palestine that can draw as many as 120 people.

One of his regulars is Issa Abu Dayeh, aged 74.

"Last Friday we were around a hundred people, ladies and young men—I'm the only old one!" says Abu Dayeh. "I love it, the wilderness, the trees, open nature. We pay very little, only around ten dollars to cover the bus."

Jaser is clear about his motivation.

"I want Palestinians to walk throughout the land, not just a kilometre or two outside their city," he says. "That's my priority—to show people the vast open spaces."

* * *

Near Rashaydeh village southeast of Bethlehem stretches a striated wilderness of canyons and scree slopes. This patch of highland desert—a rarity for Palestine—leads out to cliffs that gaze east directly into a breathtaking sunrise over the Dead Sea. It's gaining renown as a weekend getaway.

"Lots of people go onto my Facebook page asking about these landscapes. 'Can we really go there?' 'Do we need a permit?' 'Is it safe?' These are Palestinians from Hebron or Nablus. They have no idea such places even exist in Palestine," says Farhan Ali Rashaydeh, a guide from the local bedouin community. "It's only in the last couple of years that Palestinians have started coming. Now, month by month, you can count more and more of them. They are amazed by it all. 'Oh wow, this is our country, this is a magic place.' I see the relationship between these people and the land deepen while they're here."

The impact of online networking is being felt everywhere.

In Battir I met Sabrina Zaben, out for a country walk with her partner Ahmed Abu Haniya and two children. "When I have a chance I like to walk here. It's easier than before, by following social media—there are lots of hiking groups online," she told me.

"Social media lets people come together and plan something, it's becoming much simpler," hiker Joudeh Abu Saad told me, resting outside Bethlehem with friends after a day's walk.

Nearby, one of his companions piped up: "We're creating our own story. Facebook is the only way I could have found my way here."

For Mark Khano, the last few years have seen a happy coming-together of influences.

"Masar Ibrahim began focused on foreign tourism, but inadvertently also started the ball rolling domestically. All this new growth is connected with social media, letting individuals post trips online. Technology has lowered the barrier to entry for new players, creating new ways of mobilising groups," he says.

For Ghaida Rahil, programme manager at Masar Ibrahim, networking on Facebook led her to set up the Palestinian Women Hikers Club, a group of around thirty women who meet once a month to spend a day on the trail.

"We need to teach women to take care of themselves. Women don't have the same chances as men to go outside, but why should we only see the people around us? No, we should go out and experience other places and other people," she says.

After years of confinement, Palestinians are using walking—and running, and climbing, and mountain-biking—as a way to enrich their culture, deepen identity and reassert their identification with the land.

Much more than simple footpaths, the Masar Ibrahim, Nativity Trail, Sufi Trails and informal path networks in Battir and elsewhere exemplify a bottom-up, community-led model of inclusivity. They become platforms for a form of national reconciliation, linking far-flung communities together in a shared experience of outdoors.

That sharing extends to the most deprived. On the edge of Jericho, the Masar Ibrahim diverts into Aqbat Jaber refugee camp, a low-income neighborhood where in 2014, the local women's association converted a traditional mud-built kindergarten into a guest house.

"It was an idea from Masar Ibrahim, to let people passing through from Wadi Qelt stay here," says association director Jamila Abul-Assal.

The NGO split conversion costs with the community, who now have a marketable resource—the Mud House is the only lodging of its type in Palestine—and a reason for outsiders to stay.

"We know more people, we have more relationships, life has changed a lot. Aqbat Jaber is now on a par with other communities because of Masar Ibrahim," Abul-Assal says.

It's a similar story at Rashaydeh, where bedouin patriarch Mohammed Ali Rashaydeh, known as Abu Ismail, has cannily carved out a business catering to walkers and weekenders seeking desert solitude.

"First, I made just one communal tent here, in a quiet place outside the village. But nobody knew about it. I had to go to Bethlehem to tell tour guides myself. By chance, I met George Rishmawi and brought him here."

That meeting led to an offer of partnership with Masar Ibrahim. Under the NGO's shared costs approach, Abu Ismail has built a sleeping block and toilets, and brought beds and bedding for visitors. Now his tent is an overnight stop on the national trail.

"Life feels very different now," he says with a hawk's frown, and eyes to match. "Even Palestinians are coming, to experience nature and our bedouin culture. Everyone working here is making money from tourism. I'm supporting my community. I'm very proud."

* * *

After lunch in Tuqua, Yusuf Salah returned home to Bethlehem, but Hani Abu Taih pressed on, crossing the desert with George Giacaman and the group for a night of campfire conversation—and that amazing Dead Sea sunrise—with Abu Ismail.

The last I saw of them, they were setting off for Hebron, another two days and thirty kilometres away.

As he stood by the tent flap after breakfast, slurping a glass of hot, sweet tea, I asked Giacaman if he ever got tired of walking.

"Never," he said. "We are pioneers. We are opening up Palestine for Palestinian people."

And with a shout he gathered his group, shouldered his

pack and hit the trail.

ACKNOWLEDGEMENTS

Most of these pieces were previously published, in some cases by publications that have since disappeared. In every case I have indicated the outlet and year of publication in the article subheading, and given full details in this section below. I am very grateful to all my commissioning editors. Special thanks to Dick Doughty, legendary editor of *AramcoWorld* magazine, for his consistent support of me and enthusiasm for my writing over many years; similarly to Polly Hope (and, previously, Tony Grant) at BBC Radio's *From Our Own Correspondent*; Sakhr al-Makhadhi and Andrew Humphreys, formerly of Ink, for sending me to the Gulf; Dan Hayes, formerly editor of *CNN Traveller*; and Jane Knight, formerly travel editor of *The Times*.

* * *

• '"This isn't a temple, it's a philosophy"' published as 'Hope floats' in *Wanderlust*, July-Aug 2013
• 'Postcard from Qena' published in *i*, 11 July 2013
• 'Finding the Essence' published in *AramcoWorld*, May/June 2010
• 'Sugar and Spice' published as 'The foodie road to Damascus' in *The Observer*, 24 August 2008
• 'Citadel of Culture' published in *AramcoWorld*, July/Au-

gust 2019
- 'The Happy Ones' published in *AramcoWorld*, November/December 2012
- 'By Any Other Name' broadcast on BBC Radio 4 *From Our Own Correspondent*, 14 May 2011
- 'A Wadi Runs Through It' published in *AramcoWorld*, January/February 2012
- 'The Without' broadcast on BBC Radio 4 *From Our Own Correspondent*, 12 January 2013
- 'In Search of Sindbad' published in *Gulf Life*, September 2008
- 'Child of Beauty' published as 'Rx for Oryx' in *AramcoWorld*, September/October 2009
- 'Satan Stays Away' published as 'To Oman, in search of frankincense' in *The Times*, 22 December 2012
- 'Wind and Spiders' broadcast on BBC Radio 4 *From Our Own Correspondent* 'Driving on Mars', 8 November 2012
- 'To The Holy Mountain' published as 'Petra: To Climb a Mountain' in *National Geographic Traveller*, March 2013
- 'A Vine Romance' published in *CNN Traveller*, March/April 2009
- 'A Desert Memoir' published at *Beacon*, 27 April 2014
- 'Listening to the Land' published in *AramcoWorld*, July/August 2018
- 'Suffering with Libyans' broadcast on BBC Radio 4 *From Our Own Correspondent*, 26 January 2012
- 'The Burnt Place' published in *Gulf Life*, March 2008
- 'Nothing But Stories' published as 'Saved from the Sands of Time' in *High Life*, August 2014
- 'Villages and Oases' published as 'Dune Roaming: discover the real Arab culture in Abu Dhabi' in *The Independent*, 14 November 2009
- 'The Churches of Dubai' broadcast on BBC Radio 4 *From*

Our Own Correspondent 'A Sunny Place for Shady People', 11 July 2015

• 'Breaking Bread' published as 'Food from the front line: discover Israeli and Palestinian cooking' in *The Times*, 29 March 2014

• 'Wandering the West Bank' published in *Wanderlust*, April 2012

• 'Tough on the Outside' published in *Wanderlust*, May 2012

• 'To Roam at Will' published as 'Hike Palestine' in *Aramco World*, May/June 2018

ABOUT THE AUTHOR

Matthew Teller

Matthew Teller is a writer, broadcaster and documentary-maker based in the UK. He is the author of 'Nine Quarters of Jerusalem' (forthcoming 2021). His journalism is published by the BBC, Financial Times, Guardian, Independent, Times, Open Democracy, CNN, The Author, Esquire, Daily Telegraph, National Geographic Traveller, AramcoWorld and others. He produces and presents documentary features for BBC Radio, and is a long-standing author of guidebooks for the travel publishers Rough Guides. He tweets @matthewteller and tries to keep his website matthewteller.com up to date.

Printed in Great Britain
by Amazon